STOKER

THE STORY OF AN AUSTRALIAN SOLDIER
WHO SURVIVED AUSCHWITZ–BIRKENAU

STOKER

DONALD WATT

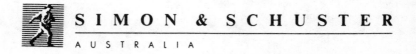

SIMON & SCHUSTER
AUSTRALIA

STOKER

First published in Australasia/Australia in 1995 by
Simon & Schuster Australia
20 Barcoo Street, East Roseville NSW 2069

Viacom International
Sydney New York London Toronto Tokyo Singapore

© Text Donald Joseph Watt 1995
© Photographs Collection of Donald Joseph Watt, Collection of Sydney
Jewish Museum,
Front cover Unknown artist, courtesy of the
Sydney Holocaust Museum,
Surry Hills.

National Library of Australia
Cataloguing in Publication data

Watt, Donald Joseph, 1918– .
  Stoker: the story of an Australian soldier who survived
Auschwitz–Birkenau.

  ISBN 0 7318 0519 4 (pbk.).

  1. Watt, Donald Joseph, 1918– . 2.
Australia. Army. Battalion, 2/7th. 3. World War,
1939–1945 – Personal narratives, Australian. 4. World War,
1939–1945 – Prisoners and prisons, German. 5. Prisoners of
war – Australia – Biography. 6. Prisoners of war –
Poland – Biography. I. Title.

940.547243092

Designed by Joy Eckermann
Typeset in Australia
Printed in Australia by Australian Print Group, Maryborough

To Joan

*For her everlasting love
and encouragement, without which this
book could not have been written.*

Foreword

On a warm, sunny day towards the end of November 1987, Don Watt turned to his wife, Joan, and let slip a secret he had been keeping to himself for 44 years.

They were relaxing in the lounge-room of their small, comfortable home at Tweed Heads, a thriving town of 35,000 people on the border of Queensland and New South Wales. Don had been living in 'Tweed' for seven or eight years. Like thousands of other Australian pensioners, he had travelled north, lured by the climate — the warm, gloriously even temperature that sits in the high 20s to low 30s all year round, even at the height of the most sweltering summer elsewhere in the state. Joan was a local girl. She was born in Tweed, grew up there and had lived there for most of her life. She had four children, two daughters, Dorothy and Dennise, and two sons, champion surfers Michael and Tom Peterson.

Don and Joan were enjoying a cup of coffee and reading the morning newspapers. They had been married for seven years, the second time round for both of them, and they were comfortable in each other's company. Don usually went through the papers first, sharing snippets with his wife, reading bits and pieces aloud to her, and they would discuss those that took their fancy. On this occasion, his eye came across a news item, just a few paragraphs long, that didn't so much take his fancy as change his life forever.

Certain things had happened to Don, way back in the 1940s, when he was a prisoner of war in Europe. He was in his early 20s at the time, and the events were so traumatic he had told no-one about them. He had built an impenetrable steel and concrete wall around them in his mind so he would never have to think about those events again, and certainly not worry about them. Only now, they came pouring out.

'Hey, Joan,' he said, holding up the *Daily Telegraph*. 'It says here the Veterans' Affairs Department in Canberra is looking for ex-servicemen who were illegally imprisoned in German concentration camps during the war. They want them all to come forward. They're going to put advertisements in the paper. It says here they're going to pay them $10,000 in compensation.'

'Oh, really? That's interesting,' said Joan, who wasn't really interested at all.

'Yes . . . I was there, too, you know,' said Don, in a faraway voice.

'What's that?'

'What's what?' replied Don.

'You said you were somewhere. You said, "I was there, too".'

'No, I didn't,' said Don, not knowing what she was talking about.

'Here, give me the paper. Let me have a look,' said Joan, wondering if she was hearing things. She took the paper and read the article aloud.

'"Death Camp Vets to Get Pay-Out",' she said, reading the headline. '"The Federal Government is beginning its search for Australian service personnel imprisoned in Nazi concentration camps during World War II, who are each entitled to $10,000.

'"Veterans' Affairs Minister Ben Humphreys yesterday announced the Government is beginning a nation-wide search for the illegally interned war veterans.

'"There are no records on the numbers of Australians who found their way into the camps but it is believed to be only a few hundred.

'"Mr Humphreys said the $10,000 compensation, announced in the Budget, is conditional on claims being submitted before Anzac Day next year.

'"To be eligible for the $10,000 payment, a person must be: an Australian veteran; have been interned in a Nazi concentration camp for a protracted period; and have been subjected to brutal treatment."'

Joan finished reading and sat there, chewing the article over in her mind. 'Why was Don so interested in this?' she asked herself, thinking the story very unremarkable indeed.

'I was there, too,' said Don, in that same faraway voice, almost as if he had heard her thoughts.

'There!' said Joan, absolutely astounded. 'You said it again. You said, "I was there too" again.'

'No I didn't,' said Don, a strange look that Joan had never seen before filling his face.

'You did! You did!' Her voice growing softer, more tender, she added, 'Come on, darling. What is it? Where were you? What do you mean, "I was there, too?" Where were you?'

Don was quiet for five, maybe ten seconds. 'I was in Auschwitz,' he said, his voice barely louder than a whisper.

'What?' said Joan, hardly believing her ears. 'When? What for? You've never told me this before. Seven years we've been married, and you've never mentioned this before! You didn't even mention it when we were on holiday in Germany in 1983.'

'I was in the Auschwitz-Birkenau death camp for seven months. I haven't told you before, I haven't told anyone before. I've tried to shut it from my mind. I saw things there that I don't even want to think about, never mind talk about.'

'But what on earth were you doing there? Goodness gracious! How did you come to be there? Come on, Don. You can't just sit there and say nothing.'

Another silence. Then, in a quiet voice, Don explained, 'I was sent there for escaping from a POW camp. I was on the run for three weeks before I was recaptured. When they caught me, they tortured me, bashed me up. They knocked me around something terrible. When I refused to talk, they handed me over to the Gestapo, and they worked me over once more. Still I refused to talk, and an officer tortured me for days on end. And I still wouldn't talk, except to give my name, rank and serial number.

'This officer was so angry with me, he went off his face. He pulled out a knife and chopped the tip off one of my fingers. He even pulled out his revolver and threatened to shoot me. And he smashed my fingers, one by one, in a special contraption, until every finger was a bloody mess. And I still wouldn't talk.

'So he threw me into a cell, and when he saw me the next morning he seemed a lot calmer. He just looked me in the eye and said he was sending me to Auschwitz as a punishment.'

There was another silence and then, with tears running down his face, Don added, 'They made me stoke the furnaces that they burnt all the Jews in —the Jews and the communists and all the other people.

'I haven't told anyone else before because I hated every minute of it. I didn't even want to think about it. I couldn't believe my eyes at the things I saw there. It's haunted me all my life, and I didn't think anyone would believe me.'

Contents

Acknowledgments

To the dedicated ex-servicemen who edit the 2/7th Battalion newsletter and the POW journal, *Barbed Wire*, for keeping former battalion members and ex-prisoners of war informed on important matters affecting old soldiers.

To the 2/7th Battalion Association and their book, *The Fiery Phoenix*, for essential background information that helped me fill in some gaps.

To the Australian War Memorial and the Department of Veterans' Affairs, for their kind assistance in checking various historical details for me.

To the Australian Association of Jewish Holocaust Survivors and Descendants for their support and compassion during the compilation of this book.

To the patron and founder of the Sydney Jewish Museum, John Saunders, AO, for his encouragement and enthusiasm for the project.

To Barbara Fitzgibbon, for her time in helping with the early drafts of this book.

To Dorian Wild, for his enthusiasm, care and resourcefulness in editing this book and generally putting it together.

Introduction

If you were to ask Don Watt to describe himself, he would probably shrug, give a shy smile and say, 'Just an ordinary bloke, retired now, but I used to run a pub in Victoria. I was also a carpenter. I was a bit of a larrikin in my youth, and I was a soldier and prisoner of war during World War II.'

A brief biography does nothing to contradict this: born at Pakenham, Victoria, in 1918, the youngest of three sons of Liz and Bill Watt, Don worked at various factory and farming jobs before enlisting in the AIF in January 1940. He served as an infantryman in Palestine and North Africa, and was captured by the Germans in June 1941 after the Battle for Crete. He was demobbed in September 1945. After the war he obtained a hotelier's licence and alternated between running his own pub, first in Bendigo and then in Castlemaine, and working as a carpenter on various building sites, until his health gave out. He was granted TPI (totally and permanently incapacitated) status in July 1989.

Yet behind these bare bones lies a story of rare perseverance and courage, which shows Don Watt not so much as an 'ordinary bloke', as he would put it, but as an 'extraordinary ordinary Australian'. It is a story that would probably never have come to light, had not the Australian Government, in 1987, decided (belatedly) to compensate Australian servicemen who had been held illegally in Nazi concentration camps during World War II.

The newspaper article about the Government's decision to advertise for these ex-servicemen to come forward was to change Don's life. It resulted in his relating, for the first time, an account of his eight days in Belsen and seven months in Auschwitz — particularly the death camp of Auschwitz–Birkenau. It is a story so horrifying that it isn't surprising he tried to forget it and put every chilling detail behind him.

The most amazing thing about Don's story is that he kept it to himself for so long. Instead of talking freely about what had happened to him, Don spun a yarn to the Service authorities, saying that he had been on the run during the eight months when he was not accounted for in the regular POW camps. Neither did he breathe a word to the people who were nearest to him. Despite a marriage lasting 30 years, his first wife knew nothing of his experience, and he had been married to his second wife for seven years before his secret finally slipped out.

For Don, breaking his 44-year silence was immediately traumatic, both mentally and physically. Repressed memories, long buried in his subconscious, came back to haunt him. He would wake up at night, screaming and sweating, as these memories forced themselves to the front of his mind, demanding to be confronted and accepted.

This book was born out of those nightmares. Unable to sleep because of the bad dreams and an excruciating pain in his knee — the result of an old war wound that nearly led to his leg being amputated — Don would go to the kitchen, make himself a cup of coffee and write down an account of his experiences. At first the words were difficult to write. He would sit there, from three until nine in the morning, six long hours, and have just one page to show for his trouble.

Then the memories started rushing back, increasing in clarity with every day that passed. The act of writing was a form of catharsis: the more Don wrote, the more he remembered and the more he wanted to write. Recognising his need, his wife Joan encouraged him every step of the way, helping him put the pieces together and complete the picture with stories of his youth and his life after the war.

As he wrote his POW experiences out of his system, Don realised that he wanted others to read about them, not out of vanity, not for personal aggrandisement, not out of hatred of the Germans, but to create an awareness of the way in which ordinary people can too easily be corrupted by those in whom the quest for power has become so great that they seek to deny their fellow human beings the basic decencies of life.

Just as important to Don is his wish that others do not allow themselves to go through the mental torment that he suffered in trying to repress memories of the horrors he had experienced. His plea is that no-one should store things up, that partners, friends and loved ones should be told, and that help should be sought from qualified professionals as soon as possible.

It has to be said, if only for the record, that this book does not attempt to be a definitive account of life in Auschwitz–Birkenau. Nor is it a detailed history of the Australian Army's 2/7th Infantry Battalion. Rather, it is an intensely personal account of what one man saw and experienced in one of the most notorious death camps of the Third Reich, at a time when man's inhumanity to man was allowed to run rampant, unchecked and unchallenged, in one of the most barbarous episodes of world history.

Author's Note

There is every chance that you will not find the towns of Auschwitz and Birkenau on a modern map of Poland.

Auschwitz was the German name for the town of Oswiecim, to the west of Krakow in southern Poland, and it is here that the Germans built the notorious concentration camp of the same name. Similarly, Birkenau was the German name for the village of Brzeszcze, southeast of Oswiecim, and where the Auschwitz II (Birkenau) death camp was built.

Belsen is the common name for the Bergen–Belsen concentration camp near Bergen, a small town on Luneburg Heath in northern Germany, midway between Hanover and Hamburg.

CHAPTER 1
Captured

I suppose it all started with the capitulation of Crete, way back in June 1941. The Allied command had taken the view that Allied troops on the island did not have enough weapons and ammunition to defend themselves against the Germans, no matter how valiantly they had fought. This was a rotten shame, because we had fought good and hard. A lot of our mates had died, good men all of them. It seemed to all of us to be a tragic, terrible waste to be giving up now.

We were given the word by our colonel, Lieutenant-Colonel T. G. Walker, who was acting on orders from the commander of the Allied forces on Crete, Major-General Bernard Freyburg, who was also commander of the New Zealand forces. The colonel wished us luck and told us that every man had to look after himself. I could hardly believe my ears. I really expected more from our High Command. After all, they were men who had been trained to lead others, but on this occasion they didn't seem to be setting a very good example at all. I didn't know it at the time, of course, but for me this was the beginning of the end and the start of what was to be nothing less than a living nightmare.

I was in Crete with D Company (we called it 'Don' Company), part of the 2/7th Infantry Battalion, 17th Brigade, 6th Division, AIF — the Australian Imperial Force, as the

Australian Army was known during World War II. We had left Australia in April 1940 and sailed for Palestine, via Ceylon (now Sri Lanka) and Aden. On disembarkation, we boarded a train, about 20 men to a truck, and travelled all day and night till we reached Beit Jirja, our camp site, about ten kilometres (six miles) out of Gaza. An advance party had set up our tents, kitchens, mess huts and canteens, and it didn't take us long to settle in. All units were issued with shorts because of the heat, but they were nothing like the shorts you see men wearing today. These were so large they hung down well below your knees. They were known as 'Bombay bloomers'.

We didn't take long to acclimatise. We were young, fit, healthy and used to working hard in the open air. By September of 1940, we had been on plenty of patrols and reconnaissance duties around Gaza and Beersheba. Then word went around that we were moving to Egypt. I remember the time quite well.

I was on guard duty, about a week before we pulled out, when the canteen caught fire. It wasn't much of a building, just wood and canvas, as you'd expect of an army field canteen, and the flames ripped through it in no time. There was no way we could contain the blaze, and the men rushed around doing what good soldiers anywhere in the world would do: saving as much beer and tinned food as they could lay their hands on. Next day we checked the tins, wondering what treats we had in store. But wouldn't you know it — of all the food that was in the canteen, our company had only managed to save baked beans! We had enough for a week.

In Egypt we were based at Helwan, about 25 kilometres (15 miles) from Cairo. It was here that our training began in earnest, with manoeuvres in the desert and mock battles against other companies. After these exercises, we would analyse what we had done wrong, rectifying our mistakes the next time round. It was good training, and we soon became tanned and lean. One of the best tricks we learnt was how to conserve water by taking a sip at a time instead of drinking mouthfuls.

The thing about being in the services in wartime is that you are never in one place for long, and we had only been in Cairo for a few weeks when, on 28 October, we were on the move again, this time to Ikingi Maryut, about 24 kilometres (15 miles) west of Alexandria. I remember Alexandria well, because I had the opportunity there of visiting King Farouk's summer palace, an amazing edifice overlooking the Nile delta and the Mediterranean, and which boasted silk rugs, marble floors and a bar that served just about any drink you wanted. This was luxury on a grand scale, and I had never seen anything like it. One soldier of the 6th Division wrote a song about King Farouk, which went:

> *And we howled, 'King Farouk,*
> *He's a bloody great galoot*
> *He's the king of all the wogs*
> *And the jackals and the dogs.'*

There were plenty of other verses and, seen today, some of the words are certainly racially offensive. However, they weren't regarded that way at the time, and the song is part of the history of the 6th Division.

By rights we shouldn't have been on Crete at all and, of course, had we not been there, I might never have been captured. But wars are seldom fought by the book. There's only one law that applies in wartime and that's Murphy's Law: if something can go wrong, it will. And in wartime, there's plenty that can go wrong . . . but I'm getting ahead of myself.

We left Egypt on 10 April 1941, nearly three months after the Battle for Tobruk, sailing from Alexandria on the SS *Cameronia*. Three days later, in the early hours of 13 April, we arrived at Lavrion, in Greece, where we anchored out in the bay. We were ferried ashore in rowing boats prior to being taken by train to a camp at Daphne, near Athens. While we were waiting, a trainload of British soldiers arrived back from the front line looking dog-tired and battle-weary. Some of our boys remarked that it didn't look good if they were bringing the Poms back. It seemed we were going into a tough situation.

We were in Greece for 13 days, living in the hills and relying on mules and donkeys to transport food and ammunition to us along treacherously steep paths. The worst of it, though, was being shot up by German planes. The Allied troops had no air cover during the whole of the Greek campaign, and the Luftwaffe did what they liked with us. We moved from our positions on 25 April and travelled by truck to Kalamata. The following day, just on evening, we moved to the beach and waded out to some waiting craft that took us to the troopship *Costa Rica*. We sailed at about four in the morning, with nearly 3000 troops on board and an escort of several destroyers and one gunboat, heading back to Alexandria and trying to get as far away from land as possible by daybreak.

Our luck didn't hold. Although we had mounted all our machine-guns on deck in case of an air attack, and had a small destroyer and gunboat escort, the Germans saw us and sent a few fighter-bombers after us. To say we were easy prey for the Luftwaffe pilots would be classic understatement. Putting it bluntly, we were sitting ducks. One plane — a Stuka, I think — came at us from out of the sun and dropped two bombs that ripped open the steel plating of the ship's engine room. Water was soon coming in fast. As there was no way of saving the ship, we had to get out and be quick about it.

The lifeboats were lowered as quickly as possible. Men scrambled down rope ladders and jumped in, then rowed to the nearby escort vessels. When the lifeboats returned, others clambered into them, climbing down rope ladders or sliding down ropes tied to the handrails. Frank Dyson and myself held back and tried to persuade the captain to abandon his ship. He said it was his duty to go down with it, but we told him he was too valuable a captain to lose, picked him up and manhandled him down to men waiting for him below. He cried the entire time, saying that the ship had been his home for years.

The exercise of getting off the *Costa Rica* and onto the destroyers took about 45 minutes, which seemed pretty good to us. By then, of course, our rescuers were lying very low in the water and had to make for land as soon as possible. Soudhas Bay, on Crete, offered the nearest landfall. After disembarking there on the afternoon of 27 April, the battalion marched to a point some five kilometres (three miles) east of the jetty, where we settled down for the night. With a few mates, I camped out in an olive grove. Around midnight, blankets and rations were issued.

As you can imagine, April can be a lovely month in the Mediterranean — the middle of spring, with warm days and crisp nights. We were able to reconnoitre the next morning and found that despite the inconvenience of being dumped on the island with no weapons, no equipment and precious little food, it was quite a beautiful place. The coastal plain rose steeply from the northern beaches and inland the hills were criss-crossed by fast flowing steams, each of them crystal clear and with colourful, pebble beds. The hills were lush and green, covered with vineyards and dense olive groves. Wheat grew in fields of rich, red, volcanic soil; there were vegetable crops and wildflowers, and a patchwork of tiny villages, with their herds of skinny, hardy, sheep and goats.

Although there were three airfields on the island, Crete was a primitive place in those days (some mates of mine who have been there since say it has changed quite a bit over the years). Back in 1941 there was no railway and only one road, which followed the northern coast. All development, such as it was, was along the north coast, facing Greece and southern Europe. To get to the southern coast, you took one of the myriad narrow tracks that led inland and up through the hills, petering out at the edge of an escarpment a few kilometres from the town of Sphakia.

After a couple of days we were issued with clean clothes, towels, cigarettes and soap, and when were had cleaned up, we went exploring. The local people were extremely poor, peasants really, with barely enough food to support themselves, let alone help the more than 16,000 Greek and Allied troops who had been dumped on them out of the blue. However, they were very good to us and helped out with a few eggs, some goats' cheese, a little bread and some olive oil. We foraged for oranges and fished by throwing hand grenades into icy mountain pools. All this fresh food after months of army rations — we thought we were in Heaven. We paid the locals for the food they gave us, but they were most reluctant to accept.

According to Intelligence reports, Crete was to be invaded by the Germans around the middle of May, with around 30,000 paratroops and a further 10,000 coming in by sea. That gave us two weeks. As it was clear we were going to be hopelessly outnumbered, we used the time as best we could: digging into our positions, mining the coastline and stretching barbed wire all along the coast. In the circumstances, there wasn't much more that we could do.

The German attack started on schedule, with a bombardment that continued for days. They bombed Soudhas Bay, sinking all the ships anchored there and knocking out all our anti-aircraft guns. Our air defence was pitiful. It consisted of two Hurricanes and a Gladiator, and the pilots put up a gallant fight chasing after the German planes. They'd fly out, come back and do a victory roll that was grand to see. Then one day only two planes returned; the following day only one came back. This was shot down the next day. Their pilots had been very brave and good for our morale. It was sad to see them go.

The next phase of the German attack was a paratroop landing, and, despite the huge number of Germans who took part, we did extremely well. The paratroops came down in white parachutes, firing their machine-guns as they dropped, but we were able to pick them off easily. We even had time to play with them. We let some German soldiers land and start running towards the weapons and ammunition that had come down in green parachutes, and shot them as they ran. They were even easier targets then. I later heard that the Germans lost two top paratroop divisions during the invasion of Crete, so it was a great victory for us — while it lasted.

Things started to go wrong when we pulled back to new positions not far from Soudhas Bay. Not long after D Company moved into its new positions, we noticed steam rising from a British field kitchen. I'd been promoted to corporal in North Africa so, wondering what was going on, I took a few blokes with me and went over to explore. Well, you wouldn't believe it! The Poms had left in such a hurry there was still food cooking. After a quick look around to make sure there were no Germans about, we started tucking in. We were really enjoying the feed and congratulating ourselves on our good fortune when, all of a sudden, a Maori soldier from the New Zealand army, who had been more vigilant than we were, passed the word to shut up and stay quiet. We were in trouble. Without our knowing it, the Germans had crept to within 60 metres (200 feet) of us, and we were surrounded.

Well, as luck would have it, we had left our rifles behind and didn't have any hand grenades, either. The only thing we could do was run, so we took off like rabbits, zigzagging back to our own lines. We only just made it. By the time we were back with our mates, the Germans were coming towards us in strength. Once we had regrouped, I was asked what I thought of the situation. I reckoned the only thing we could do was make a bayonet charge. This plan was accepted and the Maoris with us immediately struck up a *haka* war cry. We all joined in, making a terrible din. God knows what the Germans must have thought. Then we charged.

Firing as we went, we repulsed the enemy quite well. We felt pretty pleased with ourselves, but that feeling didn't last long. Not far from where we were standing, one German, who was only wounded, turned onto his side and shot one of my mates, Corporal Jim Newton, in the back. This really made me angry. Not only was Jim a mate, but he was a lovely bloke, too. I was so angry, I just picked up my rifle and blasted away at the German bastard, disposing of him quick-smart.

With another mate, Charlie Garth, alongside me, we pressed ahead for a further 50 metres (160 feet). It was treacherous work. We were under fire the whole time, with the Germans spraying machine-gun fire everywhere. We soon saw what the trouble was: the Germans had positioned two machine-gun posts at the top of a gully, and we were in their direct line of fire.

The way I saw it, we had two choices: stay there until the Germans succeeded in killing us or take our chances and creep up on the machine-gun posts and see if we could take them out. We decided on the latter. Charlie fitted a new ammo clip into his rifle and started firing at the posts, giving me cover. This allowed me to crawl along the top of the bank until I was directly under the first machine-gun post. I took a grenade, pulled the pin, waited a couple of seconds and then lobbed it in and hared off towards the second post to do the same again. A good day's work, if you ask me.

There were about 200 of us in the bayonet charge and we pushed the Germans back around two kilometres (one mile). However, as the day wore on their numbers increased and we could see contingents of them moving through the hills on both sides of us. Before long we were ordered to withdraw and prepare to fight a rearguard action.

It's amazing some of the things you recall when you look back over the years. I remember that while we were running back to our lines, and with the German planes intensifying their attack, one of my mates, Bill Wangman, and I saw a Cretan woman collapse. Not thinking of ourselves, we rushed over to her and found she was having a baby. Bill went to get some water and I helped with the delivery as best I could. People were running by all the time, not realising what was happening. Eventually an old woman dressed in black stopped and indicated that she would take over. That suited us, so Bill and I immediately started dashing back to our men. We hadn't gone far, when a bomb landed alongside us. Bill took the full force of the blast and was killed instantly. I didn't get so much as a scratch.

❖   ❖   ❖

The Germans bombed relentlessly during the rearguard action. Day after day their planes appeared overhead, dropping bombs with such intensity we could hardly move on the ground. The bombing on the fourth day was particularly heavy, and there were a couple of times when my number nearly came up. We had learnt to avoid the bombs by listening to the sound they made and watching their angle of descent. One particular day, however, I was sheltering behind a couple of olive trees when one bomb landed two metres (six feet) away and another three metres (ten feet) away.

Shrapnel flew in every direction, two lumps slicing through the tree and hitting me. One piece got my nose, breaking it and pushing it over to the right, making me look like an old boxer or someone who had played football for too long. Another piece made an eight-centimetre (three-inch) gash across my right knee, opening it to the bone. I cleaned up my knee and put a field dressing on it, but it took a long time for my nose to stop bleeding as I didn't have any sticking plaster and had to carry on fighting, anyway. I was lucky, of course, that I wasn't killed outright, but those injuries, particularly to the knee, plague me to this day.

In between bombing raids, the Germans dropped leaflets on us as part of their propaganda campaign to demoralise us and get us to surrender. They weren't very subtle; in fact, they were so unsubtle that they gave us a good laugh. One leaflet was especially aimed at the Australian troops. It read:

AUSSIES
After the Crete disaster, ANZAC
troops are now being ruthlessly
sacrificed by England in Tobruk and
Syria. Turkey has concluded a pact
of friendship with Germany. England
will be shortly driven out of the
Mediterranean and will be totally
smashed.

YOU CANNOT ESCAPE
Our dive-bombers are waiting to sink
your transport. Think of your future

and your people at home. Come
forward. Show white flags and you
will be out of danger.
                    SURRENDER

We used them as toilet paper.

We moved back to the top of the pass above Sphakia, waited for daylight and took up new positions again. It was too rocky to dig trenches, so we rolled boulders and large rocks together to make a barrier and covered ourselves with branches. Unfortunately, that didn't stop the Germans, or fool them. When they resumed shelling, they used a longer range mortar and were a lot more accurate. Another mate, Shane Whelan, was hit by shrapnel. I carried him to the doctor, but it was a waste of time. Not only did the doc say there was nothing he could do, he was so scared that he wouldn't even come out of his foxhole, and that left a very bitter taste in my mouth. I carried Shane back to our position and tried to stop the bleeding with my hands, but nothing worked and he died in my arms. That was the second good mate I'd lost on Crete and it was starting to upset me.

Some of the boys down on the beach struggled up the rough track to bring water to us, as well as a little food and some ammunition. Thanks to them, we were able to hold out for a few days, until a guide came up one night to take us down to the beach for evacuation. It was pitch-dark as we stumbled down the winding track. We were so tired that some men wanted to stop where they fell and had to be dragged along. When we got to the beach, we were shocked to see it was full of troops — thousands of them. We thought most of our men had already been evacuated and that we were among the last of the bunch. It looked like another army stuff-up and we weren't at all happy about it. Despite everything, we could have held out on the mountain.

It was a hectic night. With the troopships anchored a little way off shore, we commandeered a number of barges and used them to ferry the troops out to the ships in a shuttle service. Speed was important, as the more men we could get onto the ships in the shortest possible time, the farther they'd be out to sea by daybreak and the greater their chance of survival.

Although our battalion had preference for going on board, our commander, Colonel Walker, wouldn't move until all companies were complete. I couldn't believe it. I said, 'Come on, we're wasting time,' but we stayed there until the entire battalion was assembled. The colonel led one load of men onto the barges and was ploughing through the waves to the troopships when he suddenly turned back. I wondered what the hell was going on. Then the colonel explained.

The navy people had told him that those were the last barges for the night and that the rest of us would have to wait till morning. Well, the colonel wasn't having any of that and told them that he wasn't leaving without the rest of his men. So there we were, all assembled back on the beach. At about 3 a.m., we heard the ships weighing anchor. They were off, and we weren't.

Next morning, at about 6.30 a.m., Colonel Walker called a battalion parade. The troops stood around him as he announced the news: we were going to capitulate and were to break our weapons so the Germans couldn't use them. He said that from here on it was every man for himself, and wished us well. It was then we learnt that the order to capitulate had been given a week earlier. That explained how the Germans had been able to advance so quickly and with so little Allied resistance. It also meant that our efforts to hold on to the island had been a total waste of time. Those good Aussie Diggers who had died in the fighting, many of them good mates of mine, had died in vain.

Six of us spent the night in the hills, where we met someone who told us a submarine would be back at dawn to pick up the men stranded on the beach. Sadly, this wasn't true. We sat around all night waiting for a signal flare, but nothing happened. Next morning we went exploring and found a three-metre (ten-foot) boat and a local fisherman who was happy to fix its engine for us. We spent the rest of the day loading up with fuel, water, food, even some chooks and a couple of goats for milk. Just when we had finished, close to sundown, the dive-bombers came over again. They missed our boat on the first swoop, but got it on the second. We just sat there, sick to the stomach. Then, with all our hopes of escape dashed, we crept back into the hills.

The next evening, at twilight, I went down to Sphakia beach again with Frank Dyson, another good mate, to see what was happening. It was 5 June 1941. In the gathering twilight we could see a group of soldiers waiting along a strip of coarse sand. We thought, 'Ah, another bunch of Aussie stragglers. Let's see what they're up to,' and started to walk up to them. It was only when we were right on top of them that we realised that these 'stragglers' included a heavily armed German company. They had taken a few hundred Aussies prisoner and were herding them into a church for the night.

The Germans saw Frank and me at just about the same time that we saw them, and it was on for young and old. We didn't have our rifles with us, so Frank had the idea of punching his way out, as though it was some sort of Western movie. 'Come on! Let's fight our way out!' he said, clenching his fists. I told him not to be so silly. Anyway, next minute he was knocked to the ground by a savage bash from the butt of a rifle. Another German soldier, with his feet apart, pointed his machine-gun at me. I didn't like the look of that, so I dived under his legs to get away. This tripped him up just as he was firing and his gun went off, hitting some of his own men. Some other Germans jumped on me, bashed me to the ground with their rifle butts, then threw me up against the churchyard fence.

Seconds later a German officer rushed up, pointed his pistol at me and started to scream. I didn't understand a word, but could guess what he was saying. I had a quick look around, saw our boys were now inside the church, and decided to make a break for it. I didn't get very far before I was stopped, bashed with rifles again, and once more thrown up against the fence. The officer with the pistol was shaking with rage.

It was pitch dark by this time, and after a few minutes I thought I'd make another break for it. I wanted to join our men in the church, as it looked a lot safer there than being confronted by this madman. I figured I might as well be shot making a run for it as just stand there and wait to be shot by an officer who was clearly finding the situation beyond him. I took to my heels, running as fast as I've ever run in a game of Aussie Rules, weaving from side to side so the German soldiers couldn't get a good shot at me without hitting their own men, and made it to the church.

Some of our boys saw what was happening and closed ranks around me, trying to disguise me by putting a tin hat on my head and wiping the blood off my face. It was enough to fool the Germans, and that was the main thing. We could see through the church doorway that they had already assembled a firing squad, and they spent about half an hour going through the church, looking for me everywhere. They came looking for me again in the morning, but the men crowded over me once again so that I couldn't be seen, saving me from another bashing and maybe even saving my life. Still, I was in the bag just the same. I'd been captured.

CHAPTER 2
Early Days

I was born in Pakenham, Victoria, in 1918, the youngest of three boys. Mum and Dad, that's Liz and Bill Watt, were decent, ordinary, hardworking people who brought us up properly: to know the difference between right and wrong; not to tell lies; and to appreciate the importance of doing a fair day's work. All things being equal, they would probably have done quite well for themselves and their children, but they had more than their fair share of tragedy. They were also knocked around badly by the Depression and never really recovered after that.

Dad had his own building firm. He was a carpenter by trade and was doing very well until the economy collapsed and knocked the guts out of the industry. He had 80 houses on the go at the time, which represented a considerable investment. But when the Depression came along, a lot of people who owed him money couldn't pay. He ended up getting one shilling in the pound on the money he was due (that's five cents in the dollar in today's money), and after that he was a broken man — not broken financially, because he managed to pay everyone he owed money to, but his spirit had gone.

Mum was a jolly soul. She was on the short side, being about 1.6 metres (five feet two inches) tall, and was a wonderful dancer and a good singer, too. She worked in the hotel trade, running the dining room of a large hotel at Rainbow, in the Mallee district of Victoria, not far from the South Australian border. She kept the cooks on their toes, and the waitresses, too. Rainbow was — still is — in the middle of prime farming country, and Mum made sure a farmer could come in, sit down, have a feed and be on his way with a minimum of fuss. People didn't hang around after a meal in those days, and Mum was so efficient that they were able to get three sittings into the dining room at lunch time. The man who owned the hotel thought she was the cat's pyjamas.

Mum was so good at her job that her fame spread to other hotels, and it wasn't long before the owner of the Shamrock Hotel, at Bendigo, offered her a lot more money to run his dining room. And that, I suppose, was the start of the romance between the people who were to become my parents.

They met when Dad popped into the hotel in Rainbow for lunch one day, and they sort of clicked. They went out a few times, but there was nothing serious between them until Mum took the offer of the better-paid job in Bendigo. Dad missed Mum enormously after she moved away, so much so that after a couple of months he realised he loved her, travelled to Bendigo and proposed to her. They married in Rainbow and that's where my two elder brothers were born. David, the eldest, died when he was just 12 months old.

I was about three when we moved to Box Hill, which was in the country then, but is now one of Melbourne's eastern suburbs. A couple of years later my other brother, Bill, died. We were playing chase, when he tripped over on a new metal road that was being built, hitting his head as he fell. They were working on the road at the time and the man driving the steamroller didn't see Bill lying there, stunned, and couldn't hear me shouting because of all the noise. At first I thought Bill was shamming, but the steamroller got closer and closer, and still Bill didn't move, so I realised that something was wrong. I rushed over to drag Bill out of the way, but he was a lot bigger than me and was only halfway clear when the steamroller ran over him, killing him instantly. He was 13 and I was five.

Mum had just walked out of the front gate of our house, about 50 metres (160 feet) away, and saw what happened. She was completely shattered. I can still see the look of total disbelief on her face and the dazed way she walked over to Bill's body. You wouldn't think a single family could have that much tragedy and the grief was written in every line on Mum's face. From three sons she was down to one, and the incident affected her for years. She was still a happy person and a loving, caring mother, but from that day on there was a sadness about her that persisted until the day she died.

Later on, there was almost another tragedy in the family. To help pay his creditors, Dad got a job in charge of the cool rooms at a 40-hectare (100-acre) fruit orchard at Strathewen, near the Kinglake National Park, northeast of Melbourne, in the foothills of the Great Dividing Range. They paid him a pound (two dollars) a week plus keep and, with the way things were in Australia at the time, he was glad to get it. Not long after we moved to Strathewen, Dad was fixing a leaking pipe in one of the cool rooms, when a workman, seeing the door open and not realising anyone was inside, locked him in. The trapdoor — each cool room had one in case of emergencies such as this — was blocked, and Dad was in there for two hours before someone realised what had happened. After that, Dad had the locks changed so that they could be opened from the inside, and this soon became law.

There was no school at Strathewen, so I had to walk to school at Arthurs Creek, a few kilometres away. The town was named after Arthur McMillan, a big, strong man whose feats had made him a local legend. I grew up on one of these stories, about a cow that was bogged in the creek and which no-one could get out, no matter how hard they tried. That's when they told Arthur, who went down to the creek with a length of rope and tied it round the cow's head. He hauled and hauled, but the cow wasn't budging, so Arthur ended up half carrying, half dragging the beast until he had it safely on the bank.

Small boys love stories like that and, in a tiny town like Arthurs Creek, that story was a talking point for years. Later on, Arthur became a powder monkey at a stone quarry. They used to blast the quarry to shake the stone free by drilling holes into the sides of the quarry and filling the holes with special pipes containing gelignite, or dynamite as they probably called it in those days. After being off work for a week, Arthur returned to find one of the pipes was bent. He put it on an anvil and hit it with a heavy hammer; it exploded, giving him appalling injuries. He hadn't checked the pipe, which still had a stick of gelignite inside. Arthur lost an eye, an arm, a leg and half his stomach. They patched him up in hospital as best they could, but he didn't last long after that.

Strathewen was a good place for a boy to grow up. There were rabbits in the paddocks, yabbies in the dam and plenty of room to run around in. There was also a huge rabbit warren, and I used to set traps along the creek for rabbits for Mum to cook for dinner. It was at this time that I tried my first business venture. I saw an advertisement in the paper from a man in Melbourne who was offering a good price for rabbit skins, so I got 60 really top-quality skins and sent them to him. I was imagining what I was going to do with the money, when he wrote me a letter saying there was no longer any demand for rabbit skins and there was no way he could sell the skins I'd sent him. He also reckoned I owed him one shilling and sixpence (15 cents) for return postage.

I was ropable. I had responded to his advertisement fair and square, and so far as I was concerned he was trying to get out of the deal. I wasn't going to pay him, I was that mad, and to me that was the end of the matter. A few weeks later Mum told me Dad had sent the money and that made me go crook at Dad. 'That was my business,' I said. 'It had nothing to do with you!' He just looked at me and said, 'Son, you've always got to pay your debts.'

Dad was an average sort of a fellow. He was about 1.7 metres (five feet eight inches) tall, with a head of thick, dark, slightly wavy hair. He had a kind face and was pretty easy to get along with most of the time, although what with him being out of work quite a bit because of the Depression, things became a little tense at home between him and Mum. But Dad loved sport, particularly cricket and Australian Rules football. He played football in one of the district leagues and took out the Best and Fairest award one year. In cricket, he was an excellent all-rounder, scoring a century most weekends as well as taking a swag of wickets. I played quite a bit of football and cricket when I was at school, and when Dad saw I had a bit of potential he helped me along the way.

It was also through Dad that I met Hubert Opperman, the champion cyclist and one of Australia's sporting greats, who later became a federal MP and cabinet minister, and was knighted for services to sport and politics. Dad had been a good cyclist in his youth and was a friend of Bob Finlay, a former Victorian champion who ran a bicycle business in Melbourne. Dad taught me some of the techniques of cycle racing, and Bob Finlay presented me with the latest racing machine as a token of the affection and high regard he had for Dad.

Anyway, I was taking part in an amateur bike race at Nhill, in the Wimmera district, not far from Rainbow, when 'Oppy', as Hubert Opperman was known, came over for a chat. I was 13 at the time. Oppy had made his name on Malvern bikes, particularly the Malvern Star, and when he saw my bike, gleaming new and with the latest drop-handlebars, he wanted to know how I'd got it. I told him the story and it turned out that he knew Bob Finlay and my Dad, too, and he gave me some tips on how to ride competitively. He also pointed out that my gears weren't big enough, took out my back wheel and put in one of his spares, which had a much higher ratio.

Even though it was only a regional amateur event, it was a very dirty race. A big fellow from Beulah was taking part and he was determined to win the race come hell or high water. At one point he shoved one of the other cyclists out of the way, forcing him to crash. He narrowly pipped me at the post and there was a hell of an outcry from the crowd. I thought there was going to be a stewards' inquiry, but for some reason the officials turned a blind eye and this bloke walked off with the trophy. Even so, I like to think that Oppy's tips and the loan of his higher gears helped me do so well.

I can't remember any time when I was treated as a child. Whether this was because there weren't any other children around when I was a lad, or because my parents saw things differently, I don't know. I was always treated as an adult and expected to behave like one, particularly where work was concerned. From an early age it was my job to chop wood for the stove and the fire (we didn't have electricity in those days). I didn't think anything of it. I was never 'babied' in any way at all and had to rely on my own resourcefulness — something that I'm sure helped me greatly later in life.

One event I clearly remember from my childhood was the day the *Southern Cloud* went down. It was one of the planes built for Charles Kingsford Smith and it used to fly low over our house on its route between Melbourne and Sydney. We heard on the radio that the plane had crashed in poor visibility and that anyone who had heard the plane's engines should contact the authorities immediately. Mum went along to the police station and told them she had heard the plane, but the authorities took no notice of her. They said she must have heard the search planes, as the *Southern Cloud* would have been high up by the time it was overhead at Strathewen, and she wouldn't have been able to hear it. Mum's story was backed up by the postmaster at Kinglake, right on top of the Divide, but they still took no notice. It wasn't until years later, after the war, that the wreckage was discovered, right where Mum and the postmaster had said it would be.

Sundays were special days, especially in summer. Mum and Dad would take me fishing for blackfish, rainbow trout and eels in a creek not far from home. We would drive there in Dad's T-model Ford, park at the side of the road and walk through a paddock to the creek. One day I was running ahead, as all children do, when I saw something white under a tree. I ran over, thinking it was a rabbit, but it was a magpie with pink eyes, a pink beak and pink legs. We took the bird home and Mum named him Jack. White magpies were extremely rare, and the *Weekly Times* newspaper had carried an article only a few weeks earlier on the first white magpie ever known, which had been found in another district. Word got around about our bird, and the Melbourne Zoo offered us a good price for it, but Mum said no.

Jack proved to be a very clever bird, and before long he had learnt to talk. Mum used to call me for school in the mornings, but it wasn't long before Jack had taken over as my alarm clock. He'd walk into my room crying, 'Get up, get up. Time for school.' The trouble was, he couldn't tell weekdays from weekends, and he'd come into my room and wake me on Saturdays and Sundays when I was trying to sleep in. I'd tell him to get out and he'd walk back, 'muttering', into the kitchen. 'Come here, Jack,' Mum would say, picking him up and nursing him, 'Did Don rouse at you?' Jack would then snuggle up to her. After a while we got a young black and white female magpie as company for Jack. Mum called her Jill. The two birds became very friendly and before long Jill was talking, too. Once, an Indian hawker came to the door, selling things, and Jack piped up, saying, 'Who are you?' The man looked around and couldn't see anyone. Just as Mum walked to the door, Jack again asked, 'Who are you?' The Indian was so intrigued he wanted to buy Jack, but again Mum said no.

By mid-1928 the economy was so bad that Dad's firm had to let him go. This was an enormous blow to us because we had used up whatever savings we had and were really at the end of the line. With no money coming into the family, we moved to Ballarat East to live with my mother's sister, who had a potato farm. Dad looked for work in the district but there was nothing going, so he left home and went to work with an old friend who had a wheat farm back at Rainbow.

I went to Christian Brothers School in Ballarat for four
months and did quite well as an average sort of student. It's
likely I might have done better, but Mum and my aunt had a
falling out. Auntie said she could not afford to keep both Mum
and me, and that we would have to leave. Mum was astounded
— so much for sisterly love — but there was nothing she
could do, even if she did think her sister was being very
mean and hard-hearted. But times were hard for everyone,
and Dad wasn't earning enough to money to send any to help
us. We were in a quandary as to what to do. In the end it was
agreed that we would have to split up. I was placed in the
orphanage at Sebastopol, just outside Ballarat, while Mum
went to work as a housekeeper and governess on a farm at
Windermere, looking after three children who had lost their
parents.

I was in the orphanage for about four months, and it
was absolute misery. It was a Catholic institution, where they
seemed to do little more than hammer away at you about
God and Jesus as though nothing else mattered. They were
also fairly mean. The orphanage kept cows and ran a dairy,
but while there was plenty of food for the nuns, there wasn't
much for us. We had plain porridge with a bit of salt on it for
breakfast (the nuns had milk on theirs) and, more often than
not, tea was nothing more than a slice of bread and dripping.
They did have eggs, but for some reason they saved them up
so we could all have a boiled egg at Easter. By then, some of
the eggs were months old and had gone rotten. There was
such a pong when we cracked them open.

The nuns were always going crook at us for something
or other, and it was almost as though they enjoyed catching
us out in some misdemeanour so they could punish us. I
remember we were once on an Easter parade and, just as we
marching along the road, the man who ran the pie shop called
out, 'Would you boys like a pie?' Another boy and I said, 'Yes
please!' and for that we were punished for a week for taking
food from a stranger.

After a few months, the eldest boy in the family that
Mum was looking after came over and took me out of the

orphanage so I could live with them. That was a happy day indeed — apart from the punishments and the lack of food, I was missing Mum terribly.

It was good at the new place, and the people there were nice and very kind. There was plenty of food and, above all, a cheerful, happy atmosphere. They also gave me a pony to ride to school, and after all the walking I had been doing, it was like having a Rolls-Royce.

After two years the family finally came together again. We moved back to Rainbow to be with Dad, and Mum got a job there as manager of a baker's shop only five minutes from the high school. These were happy days, too, and I was able to earn a bit of pocket money by working in the shop after school and helping with the baking at night. And, for the first time that I can recall, I had people of my own age to play with. I went camping at weekends with my schoolmates and lived off the land, catching rabbits and skinning and cooking them. We also went yabbying in the dam.

One of my friends was a fellow called Jack Barton, whose father was a professional fisherman, with a boat and nets at Lake Hindmarsh. We would often raid his nets and take back a load of redfin to cook. One day, Jack and I sneaked away, took his dad's boat and caught about 60 redfin. We went across the lake to Jeparit, where we sold the fish cheaply. Not surprisingly, Jack's dad got to hear about it — his customers told him they'd bought fish at half price from his son and another lad — and warned us not to do it again.

I left school when I was thirteen and a half. Mum and Dad just couldn't afford to let me stay on. I had my Merit Certificate, and my best subjects were maths, geography and French — none of which would be darned bit of use to me in the big, wide world. With Dad's words of advice — 'Treat and speak to people as you would like to be treated and spoken to, and always tell the truth as it's easy to be caught out in a lie.' — ringing in my ears, I took a job on a wheat farm at Yaapeet, about 30 kilometres (20 miles) north of Rainbow, on Lake Albacutya. It was hard, physical work, rising at 5 a.m. to help feed and harness 30 work horses, milk the cows, then help with the harvesting and building haystacks. In winter I had to drive a ten-horse team to plough the paddocks and plant the grain. I worked long hours, was paid the princely sum of two shillings and sixpence (25 cents) a week, and was given two weekends off a month. I got a cheque for ten shillings (one dollar) every month, and from that I paid two-and-six in repayments on a push-bike I had bought so I could ride home on my weekends off.

After a year I told the farmer I wanted a pay rise, but he said he couldn't give me one. I said, 'Well, in that case I'll go somewhere where they will give me more money,' and found another farm just ten kilometres (six miles) up the road, where I was paid seven shillings and sixpence (75 cents) a week — three times what I had been earning. After six months of this, I moved to another farm, where I received a pound a week and keep — a man's wage. I was just 15 years old. I was lucky, but then I was a good worker. I had worked hard all my life without knowing it. Sometimes my workmates would say, 'Hey, Don, relax a bit will you. You're going much too fast.' I'd just reply, 'I'm not going fast. This is normal for me.'

It also happens I was a reasonably good cricketer because of Dad's training, and I became the opening bat and opening bowler for the local team. My new boss, Mr Dellars, was captain of the local club. He took a shine to me and taught me a few things about farm life, such as how to shear sheep and operate a diesel tractor. It was at this time that I learnt the advantages of having a tractor. My boss's cousin, who had the farm next to us, used to unhook his tractor from the machinery around noon and drive home for lunch. We'd see him doing this every day and were green with envy. 'Look at that,' one of my workmates said. 'Him going home for lunch while we sit out in the paddock, eating sandwiches among the dust and the flies.'

I wasn't bad with the team of horses and the plough, but there was one incident that took me weeks to live down. It happened after I'd been to three 'tin-kettlings' on consecutive nights and was dead on my feet. A tin-kettling was where the friends of a newly married couple would gather outside their window when they returned from honeymoon. As soon as the couple were asleep, we would start banging on tin kettles, empty kerosene tins and the like, making a shocking din. The idea was to get the newlyweds out of bed and into the barn, where we would all have a dance and a sing-along.

Needless to say, you didn't get much sleep on those nights, and after three tin-kettlings and only three hours sleep in three days, I was a bit of a zombie. On the morning after the night of the last tin-kettling, I got up as usual at 5.30 a.m., hitched up the horses and plough and set off to plough a 500-hectare (1230-acre) paddock. I had only done one circuit of the field when, because of sheer tiredness and the warming, soporific effect of the morning sun, I fell fast asleep with the reins still in my hands. The horses knew something was wrong and headed for home, straight across the paddock, leaving plough marks for all to see.

Looking back, tin-kettlings were good fun, wonderfully friendly nights, with singing, dancing and joke-telling. No-one had much money in those days, and we didn't have much leisure time either, so we enjoyed what we had. Tin-kettlings seem to have died out now, which is a pity, as they helped keep the community happy and friendly.

One summer, when I was 17, I went with my parents for a holiday at my Dad's brother's place at Irymple, between Red Cliffs and Mildura. I liked the town so much that I decided to stay. Uncle George helped me get a job at the Irymple Packing Company, which took in dried fruits, such as currants, sultanas and raisins, from the local growers and graded and packed them for the overseas market. After 12 months I was put in charge of the wiring machines. These bound the wooden boxes with wire before they left the plant. I worked hard and soon became the fastest machinist there. Before long I was promoted to grading the fruit as it came in from the farmers. This was the top job in the factory, with the top pay.

It was hard work and, naturally enough, the lads my age who worked there were always looking for ways to have a few laughs. Towards the end of the season, we had the idea of putting a low-voltage cable onto the roller-belt that the boxes travelled along — not a big charge, mind you, just enough to give someone a tingle. Well, we wired up the rollers and were getting on with our jobs when, suddenly, there was a yell and a crash and a lot of cursing as one of the packers touched the rollers and sent a box of fruit smashing to the ground. The foreman came around asking questions, but we just looked him straight in the eye and said, 'Don't know anything about it.' You'd think butter wouldn't have melted in our mouths.

Still keen on sport, I joined the Yatpool cricket club and also played Australian Rules football, both with a fair amount of success. I was once batting for Yatpool in the final, against an opening bowler called Lambeth, who was very fast and had most batsmen scared. I decided there was only one way to handle him: to go down the wicket and hit the ball on the full toss. In the first over I hit four fours and scored four more in the second. The crowd loved it. Every time I whacked the ball they started singing a song that had just become popular, 'Doing the Lambeth Walk - Hoy!' This upset Lambeth even more. He became so angry that he actually threw the next ball at me. In return, I hit him for six. This broke his spirit and Yatpool won the premiership.

There was some fun with Aussie Rules, too. Quite a few people said I was a natural, and I even thought of turning professional. I played one season for the local Irymple team and was approached by Jack Graham, a former Aussie Rules great who was then earning a few bob working as a talent scout for South Melbourne — the team that became the Sydney Swans in the 1980s. He had seen me and another local lad, Max Wallenaffer, play in a few matches, and wanted us to work out with South Melbourne in the pre-season trials. It was a great opportunity. Top football players earned good money, even in those days, and although it meant travelling 1000 kilometres (600 miles) from the bush to Melbourne and back every week, we thought it was worth it.

Max and I played well, and the team management seemed impressed. Indeed, something positive may very well have come from the pre-season trials, but local rivalries got in the way. Although they were only practice matches, Max and I played good and hard — probably too good and too hard. I remember stab-passing the ball to Bob Pratt, the top full-forward of the time, so often that I had given him a sore chest by the end of the game. I played the same way the following week, but Bob had had enough of it. As we were going off at half time, he rushed up and punched me in the back. The punch stunned me, taking the wind out of me and knocking me to the ground. Jack Graham started to fight him, but the other boys jumped in and stopped it.

I went out for the last quarter determined to do my best and kicked six goals, but Pratt was gunning for me again. He was so miffed that someone else could play well, that he gave me a mighty kick on the ankle to get me out of the game. 'We don't want any country boys coming to South Melbourne,' he snarled as I limped off. This was still the Depression and Pratt valued his pay packet. He didn't want anyone earning a reputation at his expense. I had impressed the South Melbourne management sufficiently for them to ask me to come back, but I'd had enough. If this was how they played the game in the big time, I didn't want to know about it. Besides, there was a lot of travelling involved and I had my job to think about. I also had my mother to look after. She had developed bronchial asthma from the flour at the baker's shop in Rainbow and needed someone to look after her, since Dad was working away from home again, trying to earn some money.

I'm sure you won't be surprised to hear that I was a bit of a larrikin in those days. I liked having a good time and I certainly got into mischief. I had a motor bike by then — two bikes actually, a racing bike and an AJS Silver Streak — and with two good mates, Horrie Johns and Monty McMahon, used to ride to all the dances in the Mildura district, have a few beers and a few dances, and talk to the girls. Then we would have a bit of fun, especially when we had a few drinks inside. On one occasion we rode over to Cardross, where they were holding a ball in a dance hall that had opened a month or two earlier. It was packed out, a total sell-out, and everyone was really enjoying themselves. They enjoyed themselves a whole lot more after Monty, Horrie and I poured three bottles of gin into the punch. 'Lovely punch, this,' they all remarked, and went home silly as ducks. Another time we went to a country ball at Werrimull, taking a car-load of beer with us. The beer cost us a shilling a bottle and we sold it for two shillings a bottle, which paid our costs, gave us a profit, and allowed us to drink free.

One prank that the three of us got up to was to wait until people had tied their horse and buggy to the hitching rail, and then to unhitch the horse. Later in the evening, when it was dark and time to go home, the owner would hop into the buggy and nothing would happen. We did much the same thing with motor cars. The three of us would lift a car up, place the rear axle on wooden blocks, and wait for the owner to come out and wonder why he couldn't get his car moving. We would then come along, show interest and tell them Horrie was a good motor mechanic. While he was pretending to fiddle around under the bonnet, we would lift the car down from the blocks. There was no real harm in us; we were larrikins and it was all good fun.

It was also good fun baiting the police. One of the jokes we played concerned Victoria's licensing laws, which prevented pubs from opening on a Sunday. In country towns people would sit around waiting for the police to drive off somewhere. They would then nip quickly into the hotel and buy a few bottles before the police returned.

One Sunday, Horrie, Monty and I rode over to Werrimull, where we decided to get the police out of town early by riding through the town on our bikes, making a terrible row. We roared up and down a couple of times and then the chase was on. Well, of course, we easily out-ran the police and the locals got their beer. We rode back into town and hid our bikes in the stable, which was just as well. When the police returned, they walked the full length of the main street, feeling each motorbike to see if it was warm. The next time we went back, the police came over and gave us a good talking-to. Someone had dobbed us in and the police warned us not to be so smart again.

People always talk in small towns and there isn't much the police don't hear about. That's how the three of us were busted for 'raiding' the two-up school that used to be held at Mildura, on the banks of the Murray River. We would find out from a friend whose dad was a policeman, when the police would be making a raid, and would tie up in a rowing boat nearby.

Whenever the police raided, the two-up players would rush off, leaving their money behind. We would wait until we heard someone yell out 'Police!', quickly nip in, stuff the money into our pockets and run off. We were pretty honest in those days and always gave the money back to the two-up players. It was also a case of having to: the men knew about us, and if we had tried to keep the money they'd have let us know about it. Eventually a friendly policeman heard about our two-up prank and warned us to keep away.

Then there were girls. We would meet them at local dances and also on holidays. One of the best times was during the Christmas of 1938, when we took off in Horrie's car for Adelaide. We went to a dance in Brighton and afterwards walked along the beach with three girls we had met. Eventually, Horrie and Monty got into the car with their girls, and the other girl and I went back to the beach, dug a windbreak in the sand and went to sleep. Just on daylight, a beach inspector came along and woke us up — the tide had come in and we were soaked. We had to wade back and the girl wasn't very impressed, especially as her friends had been at home in bed for hours.

That night we went to another dance and got back to our boarding house around 1 a.m. to find all the doors locked.

It hadn't occurred to us that they might lock up at a certain time, and we hadn't told anyone we would be late, or taken a key with us. We prowled around outside, looking for an open window and trying not to make too much noise, and eventually saw an open window on the upstairs floor. Monty climbed up the drainpipe and hopped in. The next thing we knew, there was a terrible scream and the light came on. Then there was more screaming and lots of heads being poked out of lots of windows. Monty had climbed into one of the girls' rooms! I don't know who was more frightened, Monty or the girl whose bed he'd stepped on. We were lucky we hadn't woken up the whole house. Happily the girls were good sports, recognised us as boarders and let us in. We chatted to them for a couple of hours before turning in, and the next day they showed us around Adelaide.

One girl I was particularly keen on was Doris Johns, my mate Horrie's sister. She was dark-haired, very pretty and a really stylish dresser. She turned quite a few heads, but it was me she seemed to have her eye on. She was three years younger than me, and we hit it off right from the start. She was a good mixer and got on well with all my mates. Before long we were seeing quite a bit of each other in those long days of sunshine and innocence. She wanted to get married, but by then it was as clear as day that a war was coming, and I didn't know what I'd be doing. We did marry after the war, however, and it was through her father, Jack Johns, who owned a pub out Bendigo way, that I went into the licensing trade when I was discharged from the army.

CHAPTER 3
Off to War

I joined up as a matter of course. There was a war on involving
the Old Country, and it seemed perfectly natural for an able-
bodied Australian such as myself to answer the call of duty.
That it was another country, England, sounding the call, and
not Australia, never occurred to me. The Prime Minister, 'Pig
Iron' Bob Menzies, had said in his radio broadcast — and I
think just about everyone in Australia listened to it —that
Great Britain was at war and that 'as a result' Australia was
also at war. We accepted this without question. Besides, I was
21 and it seemed like an adventure. I was a man, war was
men's work and there was a good chance that I'd be going
overseas. The fact that I would be going overseas to fight as a
soldier, that I would be killing people and would possibly be
killed or wounded myself, didn't occur to me for one second,
or, if it did, I certainly didn't worry about it. That's the way it
was in those days. We had been brought up to believe in King
and Country and that's all there was to it.

Max Wallenaffer and I were the first people from the IPC
factory to enlist in the army, and the management held a little
ceremony for us. We were given a watch each and Cocky
Roberts, the boss, who had taken an interest in my progress,
told me there would be a job for me when I returned, and a
bonus, too. This was good to know and was another example

of how well I was treated by the company. They had provided me with a house rent-free all the time I was working there, and Mr Roberts kindly allowed my mother to continue living there while I was away at the war. We appreciated such things in those days and, as a result, I was more than happy to stay on with them a little while longer so I could train my replacement on the electric wiring machines.

Looking back on this time, I have to say that there was no real feeling that Australia was at war, as Mr Menzies had said. Life went on as usual, and the army didn't seem to be worrying too much, either. On the contrary, they seemed totally relaxed; they were certainly unprepared. Max and I went along to the Mildura drill hall in the second week of December, 1939. Max was snapped up immediately, but instead of them regarding me as being young and fit and willing to fight, they simply took down my particulars and sent me home, saying they would let me know if I was acceptable.

I thought this very strange, but the reason was there for all to see in the newspapers over the next few days. The fact of the matter was that the authorities in Victoria, and in the other states as well, simply had no idea how to handle all the recruits: clothe them, feed them, dress and equip them. There was such a backlog in processing recruits that I, and thousands of others like me, just weren't needed. Not only was there no food and equipment for us, there weren't enough soldiers available to train all the recruits who were joining up. More than that, the army training camp at Puckapunyal, where basic training was to be carried out, was still being built. The last bunch of recruits was still waiting at the Melbourne Showground, which was being used as a staging point.

The officer and sergeant in charge at the Mildura drill hall told me to come back on 8 January. This gave me time to get a medical clearance from my doctor, and he very nearly refused, not because there was anything wrong with me but because he said my mother needed looking after. I objected to this, but I had a lot of persuading to do. I told the doctor that my mother's health wouldn't get any better if we lost the war, and that I had to do my bit to make sure we won. I also told him that if there was any fighting to do, I would rather go out and do it than fight in my own backyard. The doctor still looked a bit sceptical, but he signed the form and wished me well. Back at the drill hall, three weeks later, an army doctor gave me another medical examination. I was passed A1 and told I was now in the 2/7th. They also issued me with my Australian Army serial number: VX8006.

A few days later I was off to Melbourne, on a train crowded with so many recruits from the Mildura district that it was said if you didn't come from Mildura you weren't in the 2/7th. We went along to the Melbourne Showground, handed in our papers, and were issued with two blankets and told where to sleep — on the floor. I was also given a broom and told to start sweeping, but I wasn't having that. I gave the broom straight back to the corporal. 'I've come here to fight, not sweep,' I said, and walked out, leaving him open-mouthed in amazement.

With quite a few other fellows from Mildura, I was also outspoken on the subject of food. The army didn't have any proper cooks at the temporary camp in the Melbourne Showground, and every day a corporal would pick out one or two blokes and say, 'Right, you're cooking today.' And what a mess they made. The first meal was potatoes — just potatoes. The two blokes were given a few huge sacks of spuds and instead of sorting, cleaning and peeling them, they tipped the whole lot into a pot, mud, rotten ones and all, and then dished them out by throwing them at us, expecting us to catch them. Well, a good few of us said, 'We're not having this. We may be in the army, but we want proper meals. And you can clean this mess up yourselves!' With that we got up and walked out. They tried to stop us at the gate, but there were so many of us, and we were still in civilian clothing, that there was nothing they could do. We went straight into town for a decent feed.

Another example of the unreality of the times was that they didn't have any uniforms for us. Instead, we were issued with a khaki work suit, known as a 'giggle suit' because it only came in one size and if it didn't fit you properly everyone laughed. They also gave us an army forage cap, which you wore on the side of your head. The forage cap folded down flat and was kept in your epaulette when you weren't wearing it. Our proper uniforms, rifle, kit bags and eating utensils, came a week or so later when we arrived at Puckapunyal, about 100 kilometres (60 miles) north of Melbourne, for our basic training.

I might as well say here that our forage caps had another name — a very rude name — because of the way the part that went on your head folded down to a slit. Every soldier and airman who ever wore one in the Australian, British, New Zealand, South African and Canadian forces will know what I mean.

❖ ❖ ❖

To say Puckapunyal was a shock to the system would be a classic understatement. For a start, we had to walk there — the train only took us as far as Seymour. After that there was an 11-kilometre (seven-mile) hike. We were such a motley bunch, lugging our suitcases along the road, that the German High Command in Berlin would have roared with laughter if they had been able to see us. New recruits? Ha, ha! We must have looked more like Dad's Army.

Although we all came from ordinary backgrounds, and there wasn't a man among us who was up himself or put on any airs and graces, there wasn't one of us who was prepared for such primitive conditions. There were no roads, the water supply was a small stream that ran through the camp and, as the nearest town was 11 kilometres (seven miles) away, there could be no hopping over the fence for a drink or a decent meal. The huts were of unlined, unpainted corrugated iron, with lift-up metal shutters instead of windows and chicken wire at the top of the walls for ventilation. But they did have wooden floors, thank goodness.

There were cold, communal showers, and each hut was issued with a bin for a toilet. It was a case of 'You're in the army now.' It was also very dusty in summer, and a fine dust seeped into everything — our clothing, our eyes, even our food. It also lodged at the back of the throat, giving a few of the boys a mild irritation of the larynx that came to be known as 'Pucka throat.' In fact, the only thing to restore our now dwindling faith in army efficiency was the fact that we did at least get a hot meal and tea — prepared in a World War I army field kitchen, drawn by a horse. At least we knew the army cared! We were also lucky not to be the first detachment of recruits sent to Pucka — those blokes spent the first week of their training clearing all the scrub from the site.

For us, training started in earnest with learning to drill, dig slit trenches in the gravel ground, going on route marches and learning how to care for our rifles. Rifle practice was held at a rifle range on the other side of Seymour, and we would march there and back. The first time we marched there, in our new boots, our feet became covered in blisters and we were hard put even to hobble along. We were really grizzling about this, carrying on about army bulldust and sounding like every other bunch of raw recruits anywhere in the world, when we got to about three kilometres from the Pucka gate and saw that the army band had turned out to play us back into camp. Despite the fact that our feet were really killing us by then, we suddenly remembered all the lectures we had attended on esprit de corps and showing pride in our unit, and somehow managed to throw our shoulders back and march properly. Believe me, as soon as we were in our barracks, we collapsed on our bunks with a sigh of relief. And when we got out of those army boots — ah, bliss! The next time we marched back from Seymour there was no band, and quite a few of the lads broke ranks and nipped into Moody's, the first hotel on the way back, for a couple of beers.

Army discipline was easy enough for us to take, as we had all led fairly disciplined lives. It was the discipline of working hard without complaining, of helping around the house and of knuckling down to do a job properly, that had been drummed into us in our youth. But there was one aspect of army life that did strike us as quite ridiculous: having to salute officers all the time. Soon after we arrived at Puckapunyal we got into trouble for not saluting, so the next time our barracks went outside the camp we thought we would demonstrate how silly the saluting rule was. Instead of going along in a group, we went along in a single file with a few paces between us, so that every time we saw an officer, every man would have to salute separately instead of as a single unit. This meant the officer was constantly putting his arm up and down to return our salute — a real chore — and it made him look like Charlie Chaplin. Not surprisingly, after that little incident, the saluting rule was altered to once a day, at camp.

I know discipline is vital to an army, but saluting is a very small part of it and has never really been accepted by Australian soldiers. It's something to do with our basic sense of equality and our general feeling that if people want respect, they should earn it. There are also other, equally compelling, reasons why saluting is stupid — you can end up saluting the wrong man! One day at Pucka, the soldier on guard duty noticed a man coming through the gate in a smart uniform with plenty of gold braid on the shoulders, so he gave him the 'present arms' and was answered with a salute. The guard wasn't very pleased when he was told later, down the mess, that he had presented arms to the ice-cream salesman! He was so peeved about it that he bought an ice-cream from him a few days later and refused to pay!

On another occasion, when an official staff car was coming through the gate, the soldier on guard challenged the car with his rifle. Instead of stopping, the driver kept coming and bashed into the rifle, breaking the windscreen on the bayonet. Inside the car was General Blamey (later General Sir Thomas Blamey), our top soldier, who congratulated the guard on his vigilance and for doing the right thing. The driver wasn't so lucky and got a good ticking off.

We left Puckapunyal on 15 April 1940, under the command of Lieutenant-Colonel 'Myrtle' Walker, who, so far as I was concerned, was a first-class commanding officer, firm and straight, and with a good sense of humour. We took the train to Melbourne docks, where we boarded our ship, which, as luck would have it, was the SS *Strathaird*, the best ship in the convoy as it had not yet been converted to a troop carrier. Some of the lads scored four-berth cabins, some eight-berth. I was lucky enough to be in the pound seats and shared a luxury two-berth cabin with another soldier. A very grand way to go off to war!

Six days later we arrived in Fremantle, our last Australian port-of-call, and were given shore leave. From the moment we got off the ship, the Western Australians were wonderful to us. Three of us were immediately 'adopted' by a World War I veteran who had lost a leg in the trenches and who took us to stay with his family at Scarborough for two nights. He also took us to his local RSL club, where the beer was pulled straight from a 300-litre (56-gallon) wooden keg on the counter. As honoured guests, we were not expected to pay for a single drink.

That night, the Red Cross held a dance for the troops. So many of us attended that it was impossible to move. I noticed a couple of nice-looking girls chatting together, and a chap near us said they were prostitutes who worked in a brothel during the day. I found this intriguing and went over to ask one of them for a dance. Half way around the floor, I asked her if it was true, was she really a prostitute? She said yes, it was true. I asked her how many men she'd had. She said 105, and that her friend had had 110. I thought they were lucky to be walking, let alone dancing.

Life was good on board the troopship to the Middle East. We had boxing contests, two-up schools and singing contests, with a soldier called Ken Bridgeford doing the best Bing Crosby impersonation I have ever heard. We didn't have microphones, so he used a cardboard megaphone to make himself heard and won all the singing contests on board. We had shore leave in Ceylon and went to the races, or to the zoo, and I smuggled a small monkey back on board with me. He was a friendly creature and followed us everywhere.

We got food from the cooks and fed him in our cabin and, after a few days at sea, the little thing was finding its own way around the ship. It was good company for us and a very good talking point, and soon became the ship's mascot. But it was also a little thief. Day after day we would wake up to find an array of wallets, watches, cigarette cases and lighters alongside our beds. We'd spend the rest of the day trying to give the stuff back. Eventually we put the word around that if anything was missing, our cabin should be the first stop in the search.

I tried to take the monkey ashore with me when we berthed in Palestine on 17 May, but quarantine regulations prevented this, so I handed him over to the captain, a very decent man who had allowed us to keep the monkey on board. I later heard from some of the ship's crew that they took to the little fellow as much as we did, and his antics helped boost their morale. They were quite upset when he died a few years later.

We soon settled into life in Palestine, where we trained in desert conditions and learnt to survive on very little water. It wasn't long before we were exploring the area and having a good time. Stan Enks, a Queenslander who teamed up with Don Jones and me, told us one day that he had never been with a woman, so Don and I decided to do something about this and educate Stan in the ways of the fairer sex. We went round to the local brothel — a safe place, as our doctors took it in turns to make sure the girls were clean — and got talking to a tall, good-looking Jamaican woman. She told us to bring Stan in and said she would look after him. We introduced Stan to the girl, and I can only imagine that he had the time of his life. The reason I say this is because after that introduction, we couldn't keep him out of the place.

I have always held the opinion that, as we only have one life, it's best to see and do as much as possible, so, with Don Jones and Stan Enks, I had a really good look around Palestine. In June 1940, after going on reconnaissance at Beersheba, we paid a courtesy visit to the *muktar*, or mayor, of the town and visited the war cemetery where a lot of Diggers from World War I are buried. These were members of the Australian Light Horse who took part in the great charge on Beersheba, an event immortalised in that classic old movie *Twenty Thousand Horsemen*, and another more recent film, *The Light Horsemen*. I was heartened to see that the cemetery at Beersheba was kept in immaculate order by the War Graves Commission and, corny as it may sound, looking around there brought a lump to my throat and a tear to my eye. They were brave men, and I was deeply touched that their memory was being kept alive so well.

Another part of our time in Palestine was taken up with goodwill missions. On one occasion, the three of us and an officer were invited to visit the tent of the head man of Beit Jirja, where we were stationed. This was a great honour, and we were careful to be on our best behaviour. We sat cross-legged on the floor and, dish by dish, a complete Arab meal was brought in for us. The first dish was curdled goats' milk which, I gather, is a type of delicacy. Well, I really didn't like the look, the smell or the taste of it, and was having trouble getting it down. I cast a quick glance at my mates and saw they were not faring much better. That's when I decided to be brave. I knew it would cause great offence not to drink it, so I thought, 'Oh well, here goes,' and quickly tossed it down in one go, chug-a-lug. The head man was very pleased — too pleased for my liking. Thinking I had drunk it quickly because I actually liked the stuff, he had another bowl placed in front of me. This really was too much and I had to bolt outside.

Of course there was no way we were going tell our mates about this — after all, we had been caught, so to speak, and it was only right that a few others should be caught, too. So, when we were back at the camp, we went around skiting to the boys about what a good time we had had, how friendly the Arabs were and how really great the food was. Before long, men were queuing up to be invited to the head man's tent.

And I know exactly what they'd have thought once the food was served!

Cairo was another place I found absolutely fascinating. I had become friendly with an Arab police sergeant, and one night he took two of us to a local night club. It wasn't exactly off limits to Allied troops, but the locals didn't like foreign soldiers going there. On this particular night, an Arab strip-tease was being held, and we were warned to be extra cautious, as the locals didn't like foreigners seeing their women take their clothes off.

The action took place down a narrow street and behind a blanket wall. I can only say that it was one of the most terrific shows I have ever seen. I've never seen dancing like it. It was so good, in fact, that my mate forgot himself and started clapping. When the locals saw a couple of soldiers there, they went mad with anger, pulled out their knives and started moving in our direction. Thankfully, our sergeant friend had anticipated that something like this might happen and had a rope tied to the window as an escape route. When the crowd started charging up the stairs, we guessed they weren't coming for our autographs, so we climbed out of the window, shinnied down the rope and bolted.

We also went on a day trip to see the Sphinx and Pyramids at Giza, which was quite a way outside Cairo then, but is now almost in the suburbs. We visited King Farouk's palace (not to be confused with his summer palace, at Alexandria) and went for trips down the Nile. It was a magnificent experience. Everything we saw reminded us that the Egyptians had a proud and ancient history, and that their land was one of the world's great civilisations thousands of years ago, at a time when the people of the civilised Western world, as we know it today, were still living in caves. Egypt in recent years has become one of the world's top tourist destinations, and rightly so, with people paying thousands of dollars to see and do what we as servicemen were seeing and doing for free.

It was in Cairo that Don Jones and I tried to give Stan Enks another lesson in the facts of life, and in particular the dangers of dallying in brothels. He really had become a randy old coot, a real lecher, and we were getting so worried about him that we set off for the centre of town and a building that was a sort of venereal-disease education centre. We stayed there for close on an hour, having everything explained to us, and we thought the message had sunk in, but no such luck. Just as we were leaving, Stan turned to us and said, 'Well, thanks for that, chaps. Now if you don't mind I'm off to the knocking shop.' Don and I just looked at each other. We had failed.

On another occasion in Cairo, I hit on a brilliant business idea for making a bit of extra money to spend when I was on leave with my mates. Apart from issuing us with plenty of condoms to use when we visited the local brothels, the army also gave us tubes of blue paste. Even to this day I'm not sure what this paste was supposed to do — maybe act as a spermicide or prevent us from catching VD — but the fact is that there wasn't a single man in my company who used the darned stuff. I'm not saying we were being stupid where matters of sex and health were concerned, but most of us, when we went to a brothel, would go to the ones either run or recommended by the army, so we knew the women would be clean.

Anyway, I noticed that the medical stores or the quartermaster's stores, wherever it was, had boxes and boxes of tubes of this blue paste that no-one wanted, no-one used and no-one even bothered about. That's when I thought, 'Ah-ha, Donald m'boy. It's time to go into business!' Now, as anyone who has been to Egypt, or the Middle East will know, there are parts where, even today, personal hygiene is almost non-existent. This is no reflection on the Arabs themselves, but comes down to a lack of education on the one hand and the absence of running water on the other. I had noticed that a huge number of the Arabs we met and dealt with had very bad teeth which, in many cases, were not so much rotting as turning yellow or even green through lack of cleaning. So one day I took a few tubes of this blue paste out with me and sold them to different Arabs as toothpaste, for a few piastres a time. They were delighted and next time I went out there were Arabs everywhere with blue rings around their mouths, saying 'toothpaste, toothpaste,' so I sold a load more.

I think I must have sold about a dozen or even 20 boxes of the stuff, so I then went round to all the men and asked them if they had any tubes they didn't want. 'What do want that stuff for, Don?' they asked. 'Oh, this and that,' I said, being deliberately vague. A few days after this, a group of us were in the back of a truck, going on a detail somewhere, and everywhere we went there were men and boys with huge blue smiles and all doing sign language for cleaning their teeth. 'So that's what you wanted that blue paste for,' said my mates. 'You cunning old bugger!'

King Farouk's summer palace, which we saw while on leave in Alexandria, was so grand, so lavish and so sumptuous that you could only speculate in amazement at the money that had been spent on it. Again, we were taken there by a man in an impressive uniform, who said he was the mayor and local police sergeant. I was wondering by now if the entire Egyptian police force had latched on to the idea of showing soldiers around as a way of making some cash on the side. It was either that or there was so little crime in the country that the police could afford to take things easy, but somehow I think the former is more likely.

Farouk's palace itself was protected from intruders and prying eyes by a massive three-metre (10-foot) stone perimeter wall. Inside the wall were lawns, shrubs and ornamental ponds on a scale that mocked the desert and poverty outside. We were asked to take off our army boots and, while these were taken away for cleaning, we were given slippers made of soft leather to wear, while seven lovely girls, reputedly from Farouk's harem, showed us over the palace. It gleamed with riches.

I have heard the expression, 'As rich as Croesus,' which described the fantastic wealth of the King of Lydia, in ancient Greece, and all I can say is that Croesus may well have had a few bob in his pocket, but that Farouk wasn't doing badly, either. Gold taps, marble staircases, fabulous silk rugs, polished teak — opulence was everywhere. The girls ran a bath for us and poured aromatic oils into the water, filling the air with a wondrous fragrance. They then scrubbed our backs and gave us a gentle body massage, before wrapping us in silk dressing gowns. They were experts — at this and at whatever else was required.

We spent three days there being thoroughly pampered, having the run of the bar and feasting on fresh fish, lobster and wonderful vegetables cooked in marvellous spices. They were the best three days I had ever had, and when the friendly police sergeant-cum-mayor came along to collect us, so we could catch the bus back to camp, I felt relaxed and refreshed in a way I had never experienced before.

The mayor said he had been happy to oblige, and that we had done him a favour. 'The girls are very highly strung and they get jealous easily,' he said. 'If you hadn't come along and given them something to do, they would have been scratching each other's eyes out. My friends, you have helped me as much as I have helped you!'

We had heard rumours for quite a while that there would soon be a big push to the west, so it came as no surprise when the order reached us that we would be moving out in two weeks. Christmas was approaching, and there was a great sense of anticipation. On 19 December we enjoyed an early Christmas dinner of roast chicken, vegetables, plum pudding and beer — the best army meal I have ever had. The next day we were off, at the start of what was to be a hectic few weeks of constant manoeuvres and troop movements in the Western Desert, one day moving by train, another day by truck, every night squatting down with my mates for a meal of bully beef, biscuits ... and sand, so much sand that at times I can still taste it.

On Boxing Day, 1940, I was part of an advance party that went on reconnaissance in the desert. We were loaded into the back of a truck and driven the entire day across sand drifts and along rough, pot-holed roads to Sidi Barrani, where we camped the night. We moved on next day, climbing Halfayah Pass and crossing the border into Libya (by now under Italian occupation), before turning back, hoping all the time that we wouldn't be spotted by the Italian Air Force.

The next day, 28 December, we were off again, this time moving to within 16 kilometres (10 miles) of Bardia, where the Italians were consolidating after being pushed back by the British. With Lieutenant Steve Bernard, who had been with us right from Puckapunyal, after completing his officer training at Duntroon, we tested the Italian defences, discovering tank traps, fields of barbed wire and a mass of hidden trip wires waiting to set off a large machine-gun emplacement that would have torn our men to shreds.

I'd got my corporal's stripes by now, and Steve, as I'd come to know Lieutenant Bernard, picked me to join him on a patrol that took us right up to enemy lines. We were crawling around over stones and sand, when one of our rifles banged against a rock, making a noise that had the Italians opening fire with incredible ferocity. It only took a few seconds after the rifle hit the rock for all hell to break loose, with machine-guns and mortars being trained on us and hand grenades being lobbed in our direction.

Steve said he wanted to take an Italian soldier back for interrogation and that he'd like me to help him capture one. As everyone in the patrol retreated, Steve, another soldier and I waited until everything had calmed down, then started crawling forward on our bellies until we found a trench to shelter in, way inside enemy lines. We waited a while and then, hardly daring to breathe, pressed on until we came to another trench. We jumped in not a moment too soon, as an Italian working party was heading our way.

This gave Steve the opportunity he was looking for and he told us to grab the last man. We held our breath again and didn't dare to move until, just as we were about to nab the tail-ender, another working party came along. That made too many Italians for comfort, and we had to forget about taking a prisoner. Besides, it was nearly daybreak and time to be heading back. Steve was most upset; he'd rather set his heart on grabbing an Italian.

We started moving back to our lines, wondering what had happened to the rest of our patrol when, suddenly, we found ourselves right on top of a bunch of soldiers. Thinking they were the enemy, we leapt into action. There was a lot of grunting and punching and hand-to-hand fighting, and I bayoneted one of them in the arm. We were about to get really stuck into them, when they heard us swearing and shouted that they were Aussies, too. We had stumbled on the rest of our patrol. What a night!

The next day, two of were given the job of priming two boxes of grenades. It was a slow, tedious job that we performed sitting in a slit trench, trying to keep our heads down as loads of artillery shells were flying over in both directions. Suddenly, there was a 'whump' right next to us. Instinctively, we pulled our heads down into our shoulders, expecting a mighty explosion.

Nothing happened. Slowly, furtively, we looked around and saw that a bright-red Italian shell had landed in the trench alongside us. Thank God it was a dud! With the two of us sitting on two boxes of grenades, we'd have been blown to smithereens, otherwise. Hardly believing our luck, we scrambled out of the trench and passed the grenades on to the men very smartly.

Just before daylight on 3 January 1941, immediately before our attack on Bardia, I was sent on a small patrol to sneak through the sand dunes and cut openings in the barbed wire surrounding the enemy posts. It was treacherous work because the Italians were on full alert and one slip on our part would have meant instant death or capture and brutal interrogation.

I was under the wire, lying on my back and cutting the last opening, with a man holding the wire on either side of me so it wouldn't give a loud 'twang' when it was cut and alert the enemy. The bloke on my left was so nervous, I could feel the wire shaking. Suddenly, I got the giggles and broke wind ferociously. I just couldn't help it. It went off like a rifle shot, sending one of the men running for his life. He called me some good Aussie names later, when we told him about it. Then he saw the funny side of it all.

Just before the attack, we were given a rum issue to steady our nerves. Then it was on, and you could almost feel our excitement. All our training, all our long weeks of preparation were finally being put to the test. We charged in screaming like dervishes, with bayonets fixed and machine-guns clattering, taking the Italians by surprise.

The fighting was fierce and bloody. All around I could hear my mates crying out as the Italian machine-guns ripped into us and the mortars lobbed down, exploding in our midst, peppering us with shrapnel. Stan Enks, on my right, got a bullet in the arm, a bad one apparently, and had to be sent back to Australia. At the end of the day, the 2/7th Battalion had lost eight officers and 68 other ranks, and I'd seen a lot of my mates go down. But Don Company acquitted itself well, taking out two enemy posts and capturing about 130 Italian prisoners. They hung their heads in shame, the Italians. Some of them even felt our leather jerkins to see if they were bullet proof. They were convinced we were invincible. 'We fired and fired, but you just kept advancing,' they said.

We moved off again on 9 January, stopping about 36 kilometres (23 miles) east of Tobruk, where newspapers and mail were rushed in so we could have some idea of what was happening back home. Our spirits were high. I went down to collect our orders and told one of the men who had lost his blanket that he could use mine and that I'd toss in with him when I got back. Just before daylight, when we were about to move off, I noticed that my mate hadn't stirred, so I gave him a shake. Imagine my surprise when I found my 'mate' was in fact a dead Italian soldier, one that we'd shot the night before. My mates had put my blanket over him as a joke. Some joke — I'd spent the night sleeping with a dead man.

❖   ❖   ❖

The attack on Tobruk, on 21 January 1941, was different from the attack on Bardia in that most of the enemy positions were dug in and concreted. Tobruk was a German and Italian stronghold, and it looked like it. The enemy had also trained Big Bertha on us. This was a large naval gun that could be fired from miles away, raining down shells with deadly and silent accuracy. The first we knew of one shell was when it exploded among us, sending shrapnel showering everywhere. Three of my mates, Jack Cupper, Fred Furlong and Jack Pegler, were badly mauled in the explosions, Jack Cupper losing an eye. I was six metres (20 feet) from them and didn't get a scratch.

We captured one position relatively easily and had started to take an artillery post, when we found that its guns were trained directly on us, pinning us down. One of our men was hit badly. If he wasn't dead, he wasn't far from it. I shouted to our men that we had to bring him into the dugout, but the boys said it was too late. Then another shell landed alongside his body. When I poked my head up to take a look, there was hardly anything to see — he had lost an arm and a leg and his guts were ripped open. He was a goner. We were still pinned down when Ian and Keith Walker, both from Mildura and both Bren-gun carriers, moved in to help us out. They had the gun carrier bobbing and weaving all over the place, trying to attract the artillery post's fire so that we could lob in a few grenades and take the position. They succeeded, the grenades did the trick, and we reckoned we had done a good day's work.

The 6th Division took Tobruk, though not without some horrific casualties, and then found themselves landed with several thousand Italian prisoners. Well, we had plans for some of them because, before their defeat, the Italians had poisoned some of the wells, the main source of water in the area. This was a dirty thing to do since everyone, regardless of which side they're on, needs water in the desert. Some of our men decided that the Italians needed a bit of a lesson, so we took a couple of prisoners out with us to tell us which wells had not been poisoned. And the only way we knew for sure which wells were clean was to make the Italians drink the water.

A lot of people have mocked the Italians as not being good soldiers. I don't want to go into that, but I can say that they were certainly very inventive when it came to booby traps, and we uncovered plenty in their underground storerooms. One delayed-action explosive came in a container shaped like a thermos flask, and was dropped from a plane. When it hit the sand, the container would dislodge the explosive, which was detonated by the vibrations of any vehicle driving near it.

Personal booby traps were another hazard. One consisted of mines planted about two metres (seven feet) apart, with a length of heavy cotton thread joining them. Anyone walking between them and breaking the thread would be killed or have their legs blown off. Another booby trap looked like a fountain pen. Take the top off to use it, though, and it would blow off your fingers, hands and half your face. We found numerous boxes of these nasty things.

We also found suitcases full of brand-new Italian banknotes, glamorous stuff with big, colourful pictures — real works of art. It was money for the Italian troops, of course. We were told it was worthless now they had surrendered, so we used some to pay the Italian barbers when we had a haircut, and a lot as toilet paper. We even buried one suitcase-full, just to be rid of it. Imagine how we felt when we got back to Alexandria and heard that the money was still legal tender! All that loot we'd buried in the desert. It would have been a fortune!

Out of the blue, Prime Minister Menzies visited us on 12 February and told us what a great job we had been doing. It was good of him to take the trouble and earned him a lot of respect from the troops. He even offered to take messages back to loved ones in Australia, to let them know we were fit and well. One of the lads piped up in a dry voice, 'Bob, I would rather do that myself.' It gave us all a laugh.

Soon after that we were rolling back into Egypt.

All through the battles of the desert campaign I'd lugged a

couple of photo albums around with me in my kit bag and I was desperate to find a way of getting them back to Australia. The authorities wouldn't let me use the army postal service, so I looked out an Australian lady who was working at the Red Cross centre in Alexandria. She was returning to Australia and kindly offered to take them back for me. I took her name and address so I could write to her and thank her properly, but because of one thing and another I wasn't able to get around to it. Later, when I was captured in Crete, I had to destroy my address book and to this day I haven't been able to thank her for her kindness. If it hadn't been for that lady, I would now have no photos of my army mates, the best mates a man can have.

CHAPTER 4
PRISONER

Two days after I was captured on Sphakia beach in Crete —
narrowly avoiding a German firing squad by making my frantic
dash to join our men inside the small church — we were
ordered back to Soudhas Bay. This was a 40-kilometre (25-
mile) march over mountains, a tough call in normal times
and a terrible ordeal now that we were weak, tired, hungry,
thirsty and totally depressed. We had a lot of walking wounded
with us, as well as some men who just couldn't go on, and
quite a few of our boys simply collapsed at the side of the
road. That's when I saw, for the first time (but certainly not
the last time), the ugly, brutal side of German behaviour.

The German soldiers guarding us started kicking those
who'd collapsed to make them move, and hitting them with
their rifle butts — not just a short, sharp nudge to get them
going, but blows to the face, the head and the back, full whacks
that would have felled an ox. They also called them a lot of
names in German. You couldn't ignore this behaviour, not
when your mates were on the receiving end, and a few of us
fitter boys tried to stop it.

'Stop that!' we yelled. 'You rotten bastards! Leave him
alone! Don't do that! Can't you see he's worn out? Leave him
alone for Christ's sake!' All we got for our pains was a swift
blow from a rifle butt — in some cases bloodying our heads

and faces. After that, we learnt to keep our mouths shut, helped the weaker boys to their feet and propped them up, in some cases half carrying them, for the long march. We may have been captured, but we were still wonderful comrades.

Of course, one reason why the Germans treated us so badly was that they sincerely believed that many of their troops who had been taken prisoner had been ill-treated by the Allies and the Cretan partisans. I don't know if our side did abuse any German soldiers, but according to *The Fiery Phoenix*, the official record of the 2/7th Battalion, the German Supreme Command felt so angry about it that they dropped pamphlets over the Allied lines, which read:

It has been brought to the notice of the German Supreme Command that German soldiers who fell into the hands of the enemy on the island of Crete have been ill-treated and even mutilated in a most infamous and inhuman manner.

As a punishment and reprisal therefore it is announced as follows:

1. Whosoever commits such crimes against International laws on German prisoners of war will be punished in the manner of his own cruel action, no matter whether man or woman.

2. Localities near which such crimes have been perpetrated will be burned down. The population will be held responsible.

3. Beyond those measures further and sharper reprisals will be held in store.

 — The German Supreme Command

From Soudhas Bay we went on to a prison camp at Skenes, a further five kilometres (three miles) away. Hilly, covered in scrub and with barbed wire fences all around, the camp occupied about half a hectare (one acre). It was also a stark introduction to POW life: there were no huts, and we had to live under the trees. For the first time, I think we were truly grateful that we were in a Mediterranean setting, with warm weather and all.

There's not much you can do in a POW camp, I suppose that goes without saying, really, and before long there were only two topics of conversation: how to escape, and, more importantly, how to get more food. Just about the only food we had in this camp was lentils. These can be quite good for you, but ours had not been soaked before cooking and were still hard as stones. It wasn't long before diarrhoea was rife throughout the whole camp. Clearly, we had to find some way of getting extra food. The question was, how? The only answer we could come up with was to get outside the wire and go foraging.

The key to any prison operation, and I guess this applies equally to civilian prisons, military prisons and POW camps, is the routine of the guards. If it's immediately clear that the guards have a set way of carrying out their duties, and those duties take a definite amount of time, you have not only the bones of an escape plan, but also the basis for adapting a seemingly rigid prison system to your own comfort and ends. That was the philosophy behind our thinking and, for a while, it paid dividends. The first thing some of the boys did was to time how long it took for the guards to complete their tour of inspection. At regular intervals, the guards walked from their sentry posts to a particular point along the perimeter fence and back again, always walking at the same, steady pace. It soon became clear to us that once we had wriggled under the wire, we would have two minutes to run for cover — plenty of time!

We immediately selected a point along the perimeter that was some distance from the regular patrols, dug a hole, and started getting out at night to forage for food, keeping the hole covered with an olive branch during the day. We weren't able to scrounge much — a few eggs, some bread and olive oil — because the Cretans were dead scared. They'd been warned they'd be shot if they were caught helping us in any way, and from what we had seen of the Germans we knew this was no idle threat. The Cretans knew it, too.

We had been getting a bit of bread and a few eggs to supplement our diet of lentils, when we had a brainstorming session one night about other ways to get extra food. A few of us set up a special food committee meeting, sneaking into one hut, singly or in pairs, when the guards' backs were turned, to thrash out the subject. As sometimes happens when a few people get together and start bouncing ideas off each other, something really terrific came up.

One of us, I can't remember who, suddenly burst out, 'We'll steal the donkey!' We looked at him in silence for a couple of seconds, thinking he'd gone barmy. He continued, 'Listen, I read somewhere that they eat a lot of horsemeat in France, so why don't we steal the donkey and eat it? I mean, it's fresh meat.' That's when the penny dropped and we all slapped him on the back. 'What a good idea!'

The donkey was part of another aspect of camp routine which, up to that point, we had completely overlooked. Every morning, as regular as clockwork, a Cretan man came into the camp with a donkey and cart to clear away the garbage. I don't know why they bothered, because we didn't have any garbage that needed collecting — we didn't have anything. I can only imagine there must have been a section in the official German prison-camp handbook (chapter three, section four, paragraph five) about using local people for rubbish collection whenever possible. So, on a daily basis, we had our own garbo, whether he was needed or not.

On our way down to the gate next morning we passed the word for the men to get their army knives ready, because there would be some fresh meat coming in and we would all have to be quick about getting some. Needless to say, a surge of expectancy went through the camp. After days and days of little more than lentils to eat, the prospect of fresh meat was too good to resist. Some of the blokes were almost licking their lips in anticipation — even if it was over an old donkey.

When we got to the gate, we saw that a different man had come to clean up the camp. At first we were worried that he might not follow the usual routine, but then everything fell into place. Because the man was new, the Germans took longer than usual to let him through. They took him to the guardhouse outside the prison compound, where they searched him, examined his papers and got on the phone to check out his story. All this took time, so we seized our opportunity. Quietly, hardly daring to breathe, we unhitched the donkey — it wasn't much more than a bag of bones — from the cart and walked it out of sight between the olive trees where we were camped.

One of us stunned the poor animal by biffing it over the head with a log of wood the size of a baseball bat. Then, with us all standing on either side trying to get a share of the meat, we carved the beast where it stood. Because we had to get a move on — we had no idea when the guards and the Cretan would come looking for the donkey — we worked like stink, loading big thick steaks into our dixies and nipping off for a cook-up. Well, I've got to tell you, it was delicious. I don't know if I'd recommend donkey to anyone but, after all those lentils we'd been eating, it was a meal fit for a king. It tasted wonderful, half raw and with no salt or pepper, but wonderful, nonetheless. I have never seen an animal killed, carved, cooked and eaten so quickly, so quickly in fact that you would have thought we were professional abattoir workers.

The eating over, and our stomachs bloated from the sudden onslaught of food, we quickly washed the sticky, sweet blood from our hands and faces, dug a big hole and buried the skin, carcass and mess under dirt and leaves. The Germans searched everywhere for that donkey. They even abused the guards on the gate, thinking the animal must have got out. It was a total mystery to them — and to the Cretan, who had lost his meal ticket.

It is only since starting work on this book that I have come to understand and appreciate the enormous logistical problem that faced the Germans after the capitulation of the Allied forces on Crete. According to Gavin Long's official history, *Australians in the War of 1939–1945*, the Germans on Crete now had no fewer than 16,625 Allied troops on their hands. This number consisted of 3102 Australian soldiers, 1692 New Zealanders, 5315 Britons and 5255 Greeks. In addition to these, there were 1035 Royal Marines and 226 RAF personnel — in all, a huge number of people to guard, feed, accommodate and transport back to the POW camps of Europe.

A few days after the donkey episode, we were marched back to Soudhas Bay, where we boarded a steamship for Greece and, after a long march, to a POW camp at Salonica. We must have looked dreadful as we went along the roads, and I remember one woman trying to give us food. The German guards rushed back, grabbed her and shot her on the spot, warning the people watching that this would happen to all of them if they tried to help us.

At Salonica we were billeted in barracks once used by Italians. God knows when the place had been cleaned last, as it was filthy and riddled with bugs and lice. We spent most of our time there trying to delouse ourselves by destroying the eggs in the seams of our clothing. One bug started burrowing into my scalp. I tried pulling it out, but that was a silly thing to do. It broke, leaving half still in my head. This could have presented a serious problem, so Don Jones, a mate who had been with me since basic training at Puckapunyal (we were the two Dons of 'Don' Company), found a piece of glass and cut it out.

Our basic diet for the next two weeks was horsemeat and lentils, which is funny when you think of the donkey incident on Crete, and we all became thin and weak from a variety of digestive illnesses and bowel complaints. One man, a big man as I recall, with a particularly large appetite, really felt the food shortage. He started following a very skinny bloke called Dick Beale around, telling him he was going to eat him. This gave Dick the horrors. He was little more than a walking skeleton by this time, and the big bloke had him so terrified that he was too scared to sleep at night. Dick was so worried about being eaten that he came to Don Jones and me for help. I don't know if the big bloke merely had a warped sense of humour and was only kidding, but for Dick's sanity we had to warn him to keep away or we would give him a belting. It got results: poor Dick was left in peace after that.

Although we were in the camp at Salonica for only two weeks, it didn't take long before some of the Aussies started thinking of escaping, probably more out of boredom than anything else. The compound had a storm-water drain leading outside the camp, and we decided this was as good an escape route as any. We created a diversion by having a mock two-up game, and while everyone was looking at the pennies being thrown into the air, two or three men at a time went into the drain and started scrambling to freedom.

It worked quite well for a while, with about a dozen men escaping through the drain, until some of the other nationalities in the camp heard what was going on, became jealous and tried to get in on the act. Within minutes we had 20 or 30 men all shouting and carrying on, and that drew the attention of the guards, who came rushing into the compound to see what was happening. The guards went to both ends of the drain and fired their rifles, killing everyone inside and putting an end to that particular means of escape. We were warned the entire camp would be severely punished if anyone else tried to break out.

After two weeks at Salonica we were on the move again. Our captors marched us to the railway station and packed us into closed cattle trucks, about 50 to a truck. Greek men and women tried to pass food to us, but were repeatedly beaten back by the guards and warned that anyone else who tried to get food to us would be shot on the spot. But the Greeks, like the Cretans, were proud, defiant people and not easily cowed. Despite the warning, one girl, only a teenager, managed to pass a bit of bread to one prisoner. She was hauled back by a German corporal, who fired then three shots between her feet. The brave girl, who could only have been 14 or so, stood her ground and eventually the corporal slunk away. Had it not been for this girl's bravery, and that of hundreds like her, in passing a few bits of food to us, I sometimes wonder how we would have survived. They were an inspiration to us all.

The cattle trucks, with only the floor to sit on and a small steel grille at the top to allow fresh air in, were to be our home for eight days — the length of time it took us to get to

Germany. We were given a large jam tin to use as a toilet, and food for four days. Taking it in turns to sit, stand, lie down and sleep, we travelled day and night, non-stop, until we got to Belgrade. There, the Germans ordered us off so we could use the toilets or, more precisely, could line up and perform our ablutions between the rail lines on either side of the train, facing the station.

By now our diarrhoea had developed into full-blown dysentery. Because of this and the lice, we spent a lot of our time in the nude. We must have looked a mess, as everyone at the station just stood and stared at us. By then, however, we couldn't have cared less. Cramped conditions and a lack of hygiene, food and water had done to us what the Germans never did: taken away our pride, and left us feeling dejected.

We were next marched across to the other side of the station, where the Belgian Red Cross gave us a mug of soup each, which was very welcome, and a large biscuit made from maize flour. The weirdest thing, it was about 15 centimetres across and four centimetres thick (roughly six inches by an inch and a half). It was so hard you had to gnaw it, or break pieces off. The good thing was that when you soaked the biscuits, or swallowed them and had them inside your stomach, they swelled up to twice their thickness. They certainly helped kill the hunger pains for a while and were greatly appreciated. We lived on those biscuits, and a bit of German sausage, until we arrived at Hammelburg, in Bavaria, where some French POWs had a good, hot meal ready for us.

It was at Hammelburg that we saw for the first time what was happening to the Jewish people in Germany. We were getting off the train and stretching our legs on the platform, when another train came in loaded with Jewish women and children. We knew they were Jewish, because they were wearing a yellow Star of David on their clothes and in some cases had the word *Jude* stitched on them as well. They were taken off the train and were so filthy dirty it seemed they hadn't been able to wash or shower for days. They certainly hadn't been fed. The guards threw loaves of bread to them, and they literally fought each other to get a piece. Shocking to watch, there was almost a stampede to get to the bread, and many women and children were trampled underfoot and crushed to death. We had never, in the whole of our lives, seen anything like it. We could only stand there, powerless to put a stop to the appalling scene we were witnessing.

From the station we were marched about 10 kilometres (six miles) to Stalag 13C, a POW camp that held French, Yugoslav and Russian prisoners. The guards took our clothes and boots and allowed us a welcome shower, after which we were given French uniforms to wear. Instead of boots or shoes, we were all issued with wooden clogs and some bits of rag to wrap around our feet as socks. We soon found out that Stalag 13C was a work camp, where we were expected to earn our keep one way or another. However, we were so weak and exhausted that they let us rest for two weeks to try to build up our strength — not that there was much chance of that. Food remained our biggest concern, with a shared single loaf of bread and a small piece of cheese or *Blutwurst* (German blood sausage) each constituting a daily meal for eight men. The bread tasted as though it was full of preservatives, and someone said the cheese was made from potatoes; it certainly had a dreadful smell.

This continued to be our diet, even when we were judged fit enough to be set to work and sent out in gangs of 30 to work on the roads around Weisbach, a village about one kilometre from the camp. This, of course, was why our boots and socks were taken away: working outside made escaping all too easy, and we had been issued with clogs as a deterrent to trying. Apart from the morsels of bread, sweaty cheese and mouldy sausage that came our way, the only other food we had was a ladleful of potato and swede soup when we returned to our huts for the night. Again food became a problem.

In fact, food became of such overriding concern to us that there were riots in some huts if there was the smallest difference in the size of a slice of bread. Fights even broke out over the crumbs. The loaves weren't the standard Australian size, but something much smaller, measuring about 20 centimetres long by ten centimetres thick (eight inches by

four inches). Shared among eight men, this meant that each
got only a single two-centimetre (one-inch) slice a day. It got
to the stage where we would watch like hawks while the bread
was being carved. This often became too much for the man
doing the carving. 'Come on lads, give me a break,' he'd say.
Eventually we drew up a roster for carving the bread, each
man taking his turn and being allowed to keep the crumbs.

The Germans worked us incredibly hard. One day we
were taken to build a new road up a steep hill. We had to dig
up rocks and break them into smaller pieces for the base of
the road. The pieces were then loaded into swivel-sided dump
trucks which we had to push along to where they were needed.
As I have said, it was very hard work and was really too much
for some of the men who were still weak from dysentery. Some
were so badly affected by it that they had to work with their
trousers off. One man, I can't remember his name, was in
a very bad way, so I asked the civilian foreman in charge of
us, who happened to be the local mayor, to give us a replacement. This proved to be a total waste of time: the man just
ranted and raved, waved his hands in the air and generally
abused me.

The abuse didn't worry me. In fact, I was quite glad of it,
because it gave us a spell from work. Eventually he took the
weak man off work, but instead of providing a replacement,
he made two of us do the work of three. We pushed that
dump truck for two days, just the two of us, until my mate
weakened and collapsed. The foreman then indicated that I
had to carry on by myself. When I held up two fingers to
show that I wanted two men to help me, he whacked me
across the back with a stick and screamed another load of
abuse at me. One of the men told me later that the mayor had
been in a British POW camp during World War I, and that
I reminded him of a guard who had given him a particularly
hard time. He had also picked up some English expressions,
and when I held two fingers up to him, indicating I wanted
two men to help me, he thought I was telling him to get
stuffed.

It was long, slow, backbreaking work, pushing that truck

to the top of the hill by myself and I was surprised that I was able to do it. Once I had pushed the dump truck to the top, I had to tip out the load and then hold on to the truck while taking it downhill to start all over again. I did two trips like this and then, on the third, I'd pushed the dump truck for about 15 metres (50 feet), when my back gave out under the strain. My feet went from under me and the truck rolled over me, nearly breaking my back and giving me various cuts and bruises.

I was taken back to the camp in terrible pain, but it was three months before the guards got a doctor to see me. Not only did I have bad cuts and deep bruising from where the dump truck had run over my back, but there was something wrong with a couple of vertebrae. If that wasn't enough, all the physical strain had opened up the wound in my knee that had been cut to the bone by shrapnel on Crete. On top of that, the icing on the cake you might say, the doctor said I had a hernia and needed urgent hospital treatment. I was a mess.

Reluctantly, the camp administration gave permission for me to go to hospital. A week later I was bundled off, and I do mean bundled. Despite my injuries and the number of trucks that were available for transport, the guards made me walk ten kilometres (six miles) to the railway station. What with my back and the hernia, I was nearly doubled up with pain, my head almost on my knees. Eventually, after a lot of travelling and a great deal of walking, I was taken to the POW hospital at Ebelsbach, where an English doctor was in charge.

'Your hernia's a bad one, chum,' the doctor said, after giving me a thorough examination. 'We can fix up your leg and put your back in a plaster cast, but your hernia is another matter. You need an operation urgently, and I do mean urgently, or you will have trouble for the rest of your life.

'However, we have two problems. One, the only qualified surgeon is a Russian officer who speaks very little English, although I'm sure he would be happy to carry out the operation. Two, we don't have any anaesthetic to knock you out with. So if you have the op — and take my word that it's urgent and you need it — you will feel everything.'

I was in so much pain, I told them to go ahead and do the operation. After all, what did I have to lose? I was already suffering, so what difference did a bit more make? I was taken to the operating room, where I was strapped to a table, ankles, legs, chest and arms. The two doctors again checked that I was happy to go without anaesthetic. I asked for a minute or two to psych myself up and started to think about the good times I'd had before I enlisted for the war.

Then I gave them the nod, and they put a thick stick in my mouth to bite on. They were about to rig up a blanket in front of my face so I wouldn't see what was going on, when I told them not to bother.

'Don't do that, Doc,' I said. 'I want to watch you blokes and see what you're doing. I mean, someone has to keep an eye on you and it might as well be me. After all, you might make a mistake.' This made everyone feel more at ease — me too, come to think of it.

Not only did they have no anaesthetic at that hospital, they didn't have anything for the stitches, either. So, instead of sewing me up in the normal way, they formed a pyramid of small sandbags on my stomach to hold the sides of the wound together. I was like that for a week, lying flat on my back, unable to move, and with a huge weight bearing down on my stomach. It did the trick, however, and the wound soon started to heal.

It was just my luck, of course, that complications set in with my leg and back just as my stomach was recovering nicely. Clots developed in my right leg because my knee wasn't draining properly, and they had to put the leg in a plaster cast. Three weeks later, this had to be ripped off in a hurry and replaced with a new one, because lice had got in between the leg and the plaster and were eating the leg, causing a terrible smell. Then the same thing happened to the plaster on my back. By the time they took the plaster off, my back was red raw. Eventually, my leg came good, but there was nothing more they could for my back. I was discharged from the hospital and sent back to Stalag 13C.

Life was a bit better when I returned. The road work had finished and the men were now labouring on nearby farms, where they were well treated and had the added bonus of new-laid eggs each day. The camp administration had agreed to the International Red Cross carrying out inspections, and food parcels had started to arrive. This was an enormous help to the men, and for me it was a godsend. Because of my back, I had refused to work and the Germans had their eye on me. Their attitude was that if you didn't work, you didn't eat, so things had been looking grim. With the arrival of the Red Cross parcels, however, we all brightened up. After a while we were strong enough to think about using the sporting equipment — soccer balls, basketballs and boxing gloves — that some of the parcels contained.

One of the first things we did was organise a boxing tournament with the French POWs. A few fights had already broken out between the Aussies and the French troops over the issue of homosexuality among their troops. Our boys weren't used to that sort of thing and had been making ribald comments, which got up the noses of the French. They were looking for a serious fight and we were happy to oblige them. Besides, we had also heard that they had a few men in their ranks, even a couple of champions, who were handy with their fists, and we were keen to take them on.

The first bout was a good, clean fight, but in the second the Frenchman started hitting a bit harder and the Aussie bloke had to block his punches. The third fight started with the Frenchman rushing in and throwing leather all over the place, so the Australian gave him a few back. This created bad feeling for some reason, and it was soon clear there would be an all-in brawl if the Aussies won the tournament. Then it was my turn. I joined in the boxing because I thought the exercise would be good for my back. As it happens, I nearly started an international incident.

The Frenchman started throwing punches at me, but I ducked and weaved and managed to avoid being hit. This made him so angry that he tried to knock me out cold. I didn't like the way things were going, so I decided to finish it and, with one good punch — albeit a very lucky punch — I had him flat on the mat. That's when the trouble started.

Screaming blue bloody murder, the French leapt from their seats and started climbing into the ring, looking to join the fight. Then the Aussies jumped to their feet and started throwing punches. There was no way I was going to get involved in that lot, so I clambered out through the ropes and sat back to watch the fun. The brawl was just getting going nicely, when the German guards rushed in to break things up. That was the end of boxing matches, at least so far as the Aussies and the French were concerned.

Some of the French were really nice blokes, however, who were distressed at the way Germany had invaded their country and at how things were going back home. One Frenchman told me he had escaped from the camp and made it all the way back home, only to be recaptured by the Gestapo three days later. He was sent back to the camp, escaped again, got back to France and was arrested yet again. He was thinking about his darned bad luck in being picked up by the Gestapo so quickly twice running, and wondering where he had gone wrong, when he heard that his wife was having an affair with a Gestapo agent.

'After that, *mon ami*,' he said, 'I would rather stay here. At least I know who my friends are — and who the enemy is.'

It was in Stalag 13C that I met George Timmis, who was to become one of the best friends that a man could have. He was in a dreadful way when I first saw him, doubled over with pain and walking on crutches, his body little more than a bag of bones. He was escorted into the camp by a couple of guards who would take out the gold medal for sadism any day of the week. Once they had dragged him through the gate and into the compound, they carried out one of the biggest acts of bastardry I had ever seen: they took away his crutches and smashed them against the gate posts, leaving him lying on the ground. I rushed over to him and carried him into my hut. He was thin, hungry and close to death, but he soon recovered.

George was a Londoner, a Cockney in fact, who had been captured in France. How he came to be in an Australian camp, I'll never know. He had been wounded in the leg and foot, and had been operated on in three hospitals, each one making a bigger mess than the last. Because of the injuries and the operations, he had one leg shorter than the other. He needed proper care and attention, but there was no way he was going to get it if he had to depend on the Germans. George knew this and faced up to it like a man. I tried to help a bit by cutting a piece of wood off the leg of a bunk at the far end of the hut, and shaping it with a knife to build up George's boot. I also made him a pair of shorts from some old material.

George was very popular. A natural comedian, as many Cockneys are, he was quick with the jokes and was a star turn at the concerts we held regularly in the camp. He brought us up to date with all the latest songs and a lot of new, spicy jokes we hadn't heard before. He turned the jokes into a concert act which started off fairly clean, but then got so bad that the English padre sitting in the front row had to leave. 'Right,' said George as the padre walked out of the hut, 'now you'll hear some real jokes!' I played a drunk in one of the concerts and forgot my lines. With a couple of thousand POWs looking on, I thought it best to pretend nothing had happened, so I started ad-libbing, much to the consternation of my fellow actor, who hadn't a clue what was going on.

George also learnt to put on an Australian accent. He had a very good ear for that sort of thing. Before long, he'd learnt all the Aussie slang words and could also pick which part of Australia we came from. He had such a good ear, he was soon telling us things about Australians that we hardly knew ourselves.

On one of my visits to hospital, for further treatment to my leg and back, I got talking to a man from the Red Cross in Switzerland, who had heard how I'd had an operation without anaesthetic. He was so impressed with the result and the way

I had stood up to the pain that I think, had it been peace time, I would have become a footnote in medical history.

I told the Red Cross man about George — about how he needed professional help and should be repatriated to England, or would almost certainly lose his leg. The Red Cross man wrote all this down and I thought that would be the last I'd hear of the matter. I was wrong. Some weeks later, about a month before we were transferred to Stalag 357, at Torun, in Poland, George was sent home. That's the Red Cross for you. Wonderful people.

Chapter 5
Escape

We were out on a work party one day, when two of us decided to escape. It was so simple it was laughable. The guards were looking the other way, so the two of us just took off. We slept in the daytime and walked at night — the way you read about in books — but were caught two days later and sent back to the camp, where we were given a week in the lockup. Next time I escaped on my own and was on the run for ten days before being caught. I was seen entering a house to get some food and was reported to the authorities. This meant another week in the lockup.

A little later I made a third attempt. I scrounged some civilian clothes, put them on over my army uniform, made my way to a railway station and got onto a train. I thought I'd got away with it until a railway guard started asking me questions. I had the general feeling he was trying to find out where I was from, and he seemed to be mentioning various towns in the area: Weisbach, Ebelsbach.

'Ebelsbach,' I said, in what I thought was my best German.

The guard looked at me long and hard, then nodded and smiled.

The guard got off at the next station, walked along the platform to a policeman and started pointing in my direction.

Before I had time to do anything, the policeman and the guard came running back down the platform and scrambled onto the train. There was a lot more talking and, with everyone looking at me, the guard pointed in my direction.

The policeman walked up to me and demanded to see my papers. He scrutinised them and then indicated that I was to go with him.

As we walked towards the door, the guard spoke to me. 'Nein!' he said with a triumphant smirk. '*Nicht Ebelsbach!*'

He then switched to English and said in a heavy accent, 'You should not have said Ebelsbach. I am from Ebelsbach. I know everyone there. You should have said Weisbach, or another town!'

This time I got a belting and three weeks in the lockup.

That's when I realised how amateurish I had been, trying to get away without any maps and not being able to speak German. Escaping might sound very exciting and the stuff that *Boys' Own Annual* is made of, but to me at the time escaping was a mug's game. All it got you was a belting or some other form of punishment. It became clear to me that if I was to stand a good chance of escaping — of getting away and staying away — I would have to plan carefully and think things through in a far more organised way than I had been doing.

Back at the camp I got to talking about escapes with an English POW I'd become friendly with. We talked about different ways of getting out of the camp or running away from a working party, and the sorts of things we would need and what our chances of success would be. A few weeks after we spoke, he disappeared. I didn't know if he'd escaped alone or been transferred to another camp, but about two months later, as I was getting into my bunk for the night, I felt some papers under the blankets. I looked at them the next day and saw they were very detailed maps of the area. I was so excited, I couldn't believe my luck. Then I wondered whether the Germans had planted them on me. They had their eye on me because of my three escape attempts, and I knew they would love me to try again, just so they could give me another bashing and teach me a proper lesson. So, having learnt to be very careful by then, I hid the maps under the floorboards and didn't tell anyone about them.

Finally, the day came when we were ordered to move out. We were being sent further east, to Stalag 357 at Torun in northern Poland, about half-way between Warsaw and Gdansk, where a large number of English, American and Canadian POWs were held. It took us a week to get there by train, most of the time in handcuffs, and we did the final 11 kilometres (seven miles) of the journey on foot. The Germans weren't messing around at this camp. Apart from barbed-wire fences all the way round, it had guards patrolling inside and outside the fence with highly trained Alsatian dogs that could hear an order from 100 metres (300 feet) away.

It was the dogs, now I come to think about it, that gave us our first bit of fun. One of the POWs was an Englishman who had been a ventriloquist before the war. He had a very sharp ear and could soon take off several of the guards, even though he didn't have a clue what he was saying. He would wait until the guards gave the dogs a particular instruction and would then give an instruction of his own, countermanding those given by the guards. The dogs were thoroughly confused. For their part, the guards became so angry that they kept the dogs out until they obeyed the commands instantly, even if it was late at night. Sometimes, when the dogs were let off the leash, the ventriloquist would give the order to run while the guards were trying to get the dogs back. This went on for a month or so, right in the middle of the Polish winter. By the time we had had enough, there were some very cold, very tired, guards at the camp.

At first we took things easy, getting used to our new quarters, seeing how tough the guards were and making gadgets from the milk tins that came in the Red Cross food parcels. One man made a clock that kept excellent time, and I built a trap to catch sparrows. I was in charge of cooking for a group of four, and the sparrows were a good way of adding a bit of nourishment and variety to the watery swede and potato soup that was our staple diet. I know you wouldn't normally think of eating a sparrow, but when you're desperate, you're desperate, and these little birds were our only source of protein. Surprisingly, they tasted quite good. I also added a bit of vitamin C to the stew by cooking up a few thistles that grew around the camp. Other groups got to see this, and before long there wasn't a blade of grass left in the compound.

It's amazing how inventive we became with milk tins and other bits and pieces. By bribing the guards with American cigarettes that came in the food parcels, some of the English POWs were able to put a few radio receivers together so we could listen in to the news. Hiding the radios, however, became a real problem, as we were certain anyone found with a wireless would face a firing squad. We put one wireless inside a basketball that came to us courtesy of the Red Cross. Whenever the guards made one of their snap inspections of the barracks, we'd make a great show of gently and casually throwing the ball to each other, being careful not to drop it. Security was paramount, of course, and the existence of the radios was kept secret from most of the men. Only a select number in different huts were designated to monitor news broadcasts. They would jot down the details in tiny writing, read them later in the other huts, and destroy the paper immediately afterwards. Just to be on the safe side, we read the news to the men at different times, so there wouldn't be any set routine to attract attention.

After a month or so, an English POW and I formed an escape committee and then spent two months checking and rechecking the people in the camp whom we thought suitable and sufficiently trustworthy for membership. After a while, we settled on another Englishman, two Americans and a Canadian, making a committee of six. For security reasons the existence of this group was kept a secret, even from our best mates. It was only when it came to carrying out the various escape plans that we devised, that anyone outside the six of us knew what we were up to.

Our prized possessions were the maps that had so mysteriously come my way at Stalag 13C. To these we added other bits of information we had been able to pick up, such as the names of the railway stations we had passed through on the way to Torun, and the distances between them. We then picked two special work teams to build two separate tunnels, one at each end of the compound. We took it in turns to dispose of the dirt, loading it into special pockets made from old clothes and spreading it around the compound with our feet.

I have only recently been told that this ruse was portrayed in an excellent POW movie, *The Great Escape*, which starred Steve McQueen and Richard Attenborough. I haven't seen that film or any other POW film, for reasons that I will go into later. I've also been told there was another scene in *The Great Escape* that might have been based on our own experiences: the way wooden bunk slats were used to shore up the roofs of the tunnels. We used so many, it was hard at times to get a decent night's sleep. Many's the night we woke up to the sound of someone crashing from the top bunk down to the middle bunk and then down on top of the man in the bottom bunk.

Once the two tunnels had been dug, we built a third, this one intended to be discovered by the Germans. We figured they would be on the look-out for a bit of tunnelling, as it was only human nature to try to escape, and if they found a tunnel they'd feel pleased with themselves and wouldn't look any further. Sure enough, the Germans did discover one of the tunnels and punished us by taking away even more bed boards. At one stage we were down to three bed boards apiece, each of them 15 centimetres (six inches) wide. We used one for the head, one for the behind and one for the feet. It took a while, but eventually we became experts at sleeping in this uncomfortable, precarious way.

We were a very organised escape committee. Everyone listed for an escape had to do a training course to test their trustworthiness and survival ability. We couldn't afford to have anything go wrong and be discovered by the guards. The men were interviewed and trained not to show fear. We did this by getting them to talk to the guards in broken German and watch how the guards responded. We were efficient in other ways, too. We had special sections making suits from blankets, while other people made hats and shoes from leather obtained by bribing a guard with cigarettes.

We developed quite a cigarette economy. The Canadians and Americans often received cartons of 1000 cigarettes apiece. We used these to buy German money from the guards and to barter for the bits and pieces we needed, such as paper and ink for the false identity cards we made. Our expert here was an English POW who had been a commercial traveller in Germany before the war. He did a very good job of forging official papers, which was just a well as the Germans were sticklers for ID cards. Even law-abiding civilians could expect to have to produce their ID papers two or three times a day.

We got six people out using the tunnel. Of these, two made it back to England and sent us letters containing the special code names they had been assigned; the other four didn't make it. I had my go early in April 1944, telling only my best mate, Les White. I left him some of the photos and personal effects that he was to send to my mother after the war, unless I contacted him first. It was hard not telling the rest of my mates what I was up to, but the risks were just too great. The chances were that they would be interrogated once my escape was discovered, and I couldn't risk anything happening to me or to other members of the escape team.

The former commercial traveller-cum-forger on the escape committee was really worth his weight in gold. He had an idea for an alternate escape route to the one we had been using, and he put it to me the night before I broke out.

'Listen, Don,' he said. 'I've been thinking about your escape route and I really think you would be a whole lot better of if you headed south, towards Warsaw, before heading west.'

'Mate,' I said, 'I'll do whatever you think is a fair thing, you know that. But going south? Won't that add quite a bit to the journey?'

'Yes, Don, it will,' he replied. 'But look at it this way. If you were the camp commandant and someone broke out, where would you start looking for them?'

'To the west. I'd reckon anyone getting out of here would put their tail between their legs and get as far west as quickly as possible.'

'My thoughts exactly,' he said. 'That's why I think you should go south.'

The first night I was on the run I reckoned I covered 50 kilometres (30 miles in the old money), mainly along roads, putting as much distance as I could between myself and the camp. I know 50 kilometres may sound like a lot, but my spirits were high and the adrenalin was rushing through my system. I had escaped, and I wasn't going back. At dawn I set about finding some shelter for the day and eventually hid out in a dry ditch. I ate some of the food the escape committee had given me and started to think, for the first time in months, that life could be good after all. Strangely, although I was tired after my night-time run, I was so full of energy, not to mention fear of being recaptured, that I slept only fitfully.

At first I kept an eye open for patrols, then I thought, 'If I'm supposed to be a normal, law-abiding citizen, it would make more sense if I acted that way.' So I stopped walking by night and sleeping by day, and started travelling by day. On the second day, I was walking along the road, when a German army convoy came along. I nearly died. My insides turned to jelly. 'This is it,' I thought, 'I'm a dead duck.'

Some of the soldiers in the trucks called out to me. I didn't have a clue what they were saying, so I just smiled and waved at them. The convoy didn't stop and I heaved a mighty sigh of relief.

On the third day, I arrived in Plonsk, about 30 kilometres (20 miles) north of Warsaw, and decided to risk buying a train ticket to Warsaw. It went like a dream. I handed over my documents, but the man at the counter barely looked at them. He asked me some questions, in Polish of course, and I handed over a letter from my 'doctor' that the escape committee had prepared for eventualities like this. Looking back, I think this letter did more to save me than any other document.

Back at Torun, we had decided that there was no way my pidgin German was going to get me very far, and I couldn't run the risk of being caught out on a matter of geography, they way I had during one of my escapes from Stalag 13C. So we wrote this wonderful letter from a doctor in Heidelberg, who testified that I had sustained some sort of weird and mysterious throat injury while fighting for the Reich, and had lost my ability to speak. Although it was hoped I would be able to speak in a few months, so grave were the injuries that I might never speak again.

The letter was a beauty, written on official-looking letterhead by a 'doctor' with lots of letters after his name. It wasn't just a beauty, it was magnificent, fooling not only every railway guard I had to deal with, but any number of random inspections by German soldiers, police and even the Gestapo. All my other documents had been carefully prepared to complement each other and present me as a loyal German who had suffered while fighting gallantly for his country.

According to my false ID card, I was Karl Schneider from Heidelberg, and was on my way to visit my frail old mother back home. The fact that I was quite tall — 1.78 m (five foot ten inches) and had a blond hair and an easy smile, simply added to the picture of me as a bright-eyed Aryan, the epitome of Teutonic manhood, the pride of Nazi Germany.

The ruse worked extremely well. Wearing civilian clothes made from blankets by the escape-committee tailor, and with a German hat, briefcase and shoes obtained by bartering a couple of cartons of cigarettes, I looked exactly what my documents proclaimed me as being. Whenever anyone tried to engage me in conversation, I pointed to my throat and made signs that I could not talk. When they smiled in acknowledgment, it steadied my nerves. When they talked among themselves, I pretended to listen and take interest. When they laughed, clearly because someone had made a joke, I smiled along with them.

The escape committee had given me plenty of money, and in small denominations so as not to attract attention. When it came to buying food at railway stations, I simply pointed to what I wanted and handed over a couple of notes. Geed up by my success, I even carried on the ruse while on the run through the countryside. I'd knock at a farmhouse door, raise my hat politely, hand over the letter from my doctor and make signs for wanting food and drink. One woman, I suppose she must have been the farmer's wife, was so taken in that she carved me off a lump of German sausage and two thick slices of freshly home-made bread. I even sat down in her kitchen to eat it so I wouldn't seem suspicious. I offered her money, but she shook her head. I smiled my thanks and went on my way, uttering a silent prayer that I had got away with it again.

Growing more confident with every day that I was on the run, I even knocked on farmhouse doors and indicated I wanted to sleep in the barn. One farmer and his wife invited me inside and gave me a meal of boiled potatoes, smoked pork and sauerkraut (I ate every mouthful) and then asked if I would like to sleep upstairs. I thought this would be pushing my luck and pointed to the barn. They smiled and showed me the way. Next morning, they gave me breakfast and a couple of thick slices of black bread and two big slices of smoked pork to take with me. My spirits were soaring.

Although it went very well, travelling by train, and covering an enormous distance every day, I was still living on my wits. It was utterly exhausting and was, beyond any doubt, the most nerve-racking experience of my life. The first time the Gestapo got on the train to check tickets and ID papers, my insides went to water. I'm sure the blood must have drained from my face when I handed over my papers and the letter from my 'doctor', but then everyone was intimidated by the Gestapo. I soon realised that even ordinary people, Germans and Poles with nothing to hide, would go quiet and pale when the secret police came along. Once that penny had dropped, I felt more confident that I wouldn't give myself away.

Warsaw was so big that it took me a while to get out of the city. However, I stuck to the main roads, where there were plenty of people, and tried to put on a confident air no matter how my insides were churning. After Warsaw, I made a point of varying my means of travel, sometimes taking a train for two or three days at a time, sometimes walking for two or three days, scrounging food, sleeping in haystacks and under bridges. I used the sun and my wrist-watch as a compass (yes, I'd been able to hold on to my watch, hiding it in different places all the time), and got lifts on bullock carts and horse-drawn buggies, so that anyone who might have been the least bit suspicious would have a hard job knowing where to look for me.

It's only since I have been compiling these memoirs that I have bothered to look at an atlas and see where my journey took me. I'm amazed to see how far I travelled. My escape map was very simplified, showing towns rather than distances, and even though I'd been good at geography at school, there was no way I could keep track of the distances I was covering. With Warsaw behind me, I headed south, through Radom, Kielce, Czestochowa and Katowice, then across the border into Czechoslovakia, and on to Olomouc and Brno, where I turned west and headed for Jihlava and Prague.

I got off the train at Prague and hung around the railway station for a while, wondering what to do next. I checked the railway timetable and saw that there wasn't a train for Pilsen, the next town on my map, for several hours. As Prague was a major city, the main railway station was full of people, with soldiers everywhere. I didn't feel safe hanging around, possibly drawing attention to myself, so after some food and a cup of coffee at a station stall, I pressed on, on foot, using the sun for direction. It took me two days to walk to Pilsen. There, I went straight to the railway station and waited for a train to take me over the Czechoslovak border into Germany and on to Nuremberg and Wiesloch, a small town south of Heidelberg. From Wiesloch I was to turn south, following the River Rhine towards Switzerland.

I took a train to Freiburg, a pretty town in the Black Forest, and then started walking again, always south, towards a freedom that was now so near I could almost taste it. My escape map only went as far as Freiburg, so I was now on my own. Outside the town I got a lift on a bullock cart with a farmer who took me home and gave me some bread and a couple of thick slices of home-cured pork. Then I continued south to Mulhouse, where I went to the railway station to get my bearings. I have heard that in England during the war, all road signs were taken down because of the fear of invasion. Well, there were no such fears in Germany, and every railway station had a wall-map of the region. This was always a big help to me. I had a wash and a shave at the station and set off again, walking until dark. I then had a small meal of some scraps of food that I had been able to hang on to, and went to sleep in a paddock under some trees.

Next morning I was really excited. I had been on the run for exactly 20 days and now, finally, the Swiss border was so close I felt I could reach out and touch it. I had travelled nearly 1500 kilometres (1000 miles) without being detected, and I knew I was going to succeed. I called in at two more homes for bread and sausage, then pressed on. My spirits were soaring.

Being so close to Switzerland, a neutral country that was taking no part in the war, I guessed the Germans would have massive patrols along every road that led to the border, so I decided to cut across country, where I figured it would be safer. I was now in the foothills of the Alps, where winter snow was still falling. This made progress very difficult. I couldn't see the dips and potholes and fell over several times. I hadn't planned on this, so, as darkness fell, I burrowed into a drift of soft snow, thinking it would keep me warm. How wrong can you be! I barely slept at all that night, I was shivering so much. I got up early the next morning, washed in an ice-cold stream and had a good drink of water, before heading uphill to get my bearings.

I had no idea the going would be as tough as this. It was so difficult, walking in ordinary shoes through thick drifts of snow, that I seemed to be making no progress at all. Then, on my third day in the mountains, I noticed a road snaking way down beneath me. By my calculations, I was now one or two kilometres (about one mile) inside Switzerland, so I kept my eyes open for a Swiss border patrol — I was sure they would

Escape route from Stalag 357

have one. I hit the road and headed south and, after an hour or so, I saw a uniformed patrol up ahead. I was so pleased to see them that I threw my arms in the air and walked along the middle of the road towards them. It was only as I drew closer that I realised they weren't Swiss at all. They were Germans.

I didn't know how many kilometres I had covered in the past three days, going uphill and down dale, but I had totally lost my bearings in the mountains, where the German, French and Swiss borders run together. Instead of being home free in Switzerland, I had handed myself back to the enemy. All that ducking and hiding, and travelling and agonising over whether I would be captured, all that living on my nerves for days at a time, had come to nothing. I felt so sick in the stomach that I couldn't have cared less if they had shot me on the spot. I figured I deserved it for being so bloody careless.

It was 26 April 1944, exactly three weeks after I'd broken out of Stalag 357, and I was a prisoner again. The soldiers took me to an interrogation centre, where I stuck to the voice trick, played dumb and said nothing. They screamed at me, calling me a traitor. My documents were so good that they believed them completely and took me for a German trying to escape to Switzerland. Boy, was I pleased — if they had known I was Australian they would also have known that my papers were false and could have shot me as a spy. After all, I was in civilian clothes and they could have shot me without any comeback. As it was, they just bashed me up a bit, pistol-whipped me, all that sort of thing, and kept screaming that I was a traitor.

Next day I was taken to Heidelberg, where another bunch of soldiers or police started on me, pistol-whipping me, kicking me in the ribs, punching me in the kidneys, the usual thing. This went on for two days, and all the time they were bashing me around, they were also checking up on me. After all, this was Heidelberg and my papers said I was from Heidelberg. I was a local boy. I was sticking to my story about being Karl Schneider from Heidelberg, who couldn't speak because of a throat injury. However, they came back and said the street where I claimed I lived didn't exist, and neither did the 'doctor' who had signed the letter saying I couldn't speak. I was running out of time, and out of luck.

Then, after half a day of them yelling and screaming at me, and punching me in the face and kidneys, they decided to call my bluff. Taking me at my word that I couldn't speak, they gave me a pencil and a piece of paper and told me to write down the answers. Of course I couldn't write German, so they had me cold. I confessed. I told them that I was an Australian POW and gave my name, rank and serial number, plus my POW number — 10418 — so that they could trace which *stalag* I had escaped from.

Well, that really intrigued them — not that I was an escaped POW, but that I had such high-quality forged papers and such clothes. They wanted to know where I had got them and started bashing me up all over again. God, I was so sore I could have told them anything — but I knew that I couldn't. I couldn't tell them about the escape committee, or how we made all our clothes and bribed the guards to get paper and ink for the documents and dyes for the clothes.

They then took me off to Nuremberg, to what I was told was a sort of regional police headquarters, where the Kripo (the criminal police), the Gestapo and German military intelligence interrogated captured Allied troops, Resistance workers, spies and anyone else who fell under suspicion. I knew immediately that I was dealing with another kind of people entirely — people who could tell from experience and a mass of information that had already been collected, whether a story was true or false.

They worked on me systematically, two or three at a time, strapping me into a chair and taking it in turns to hit me around the face and kidneys, and kick me in the base of the spine — cold, efficient brutality. They would knock me around until I fell unconscious, then throw me into a cell until I came to, when they'd rip into me again. All the while there was this officer — I can't recall his name, but he said he was a major — who was overseeing what was going on. It was as though he took a special interest in my case and wanted

Left: World War I veteran Sergeant-Major 'Shorty' Walker of the 2/7th Battalion wearing desert-issue Bombay bloomers so large that he and Don Watt could fit in them together, with room to spare.

Right: Captain H. Halliday, much-respected captain of 'Don' Company saw front-line action with Don Watt in North Africa, Greece and Crete. Captured in Crete, he spent the rest of the war as a POW in Germany.

Don Watt and Bren gun on guard duty on a roof-top in Gaza.

Recently arrived in Tel Aviv, *left* to *right*, Don Watt, Don Jones, 'Pop' Brown and George Black.

At a photographic studio in Alexandria, March 1941. *Back row*: George Bennet, sailor from HMS *Sydney*, Don Watt. *Front row*: Gordon ('Shorty') Gibbs, Arthur Bell.

Stan Enks, ' . . . the soldier with the insatiable sex drive whom I had introduced to the joys of women . . . '.

Charlie Garth, a 2/7th mate who could smell the burning at Auschwitz from a forced-labour factory in Krakow, 25 kilometres away.

George Timmis, ' . . . one of the best friends that a man could have.' Don Watt arranged his repatriation to England from Stalag 13C in Germany.

Right: The grim siding at Auschwitz–Birkenau, where wagons discharged their human 'cattle'.

Left: 'One by one, the cattle
trucks would open and the
bewildered, wretched people
inside — 100 to a truck —
would be ordered down onto
the platform . . . '.

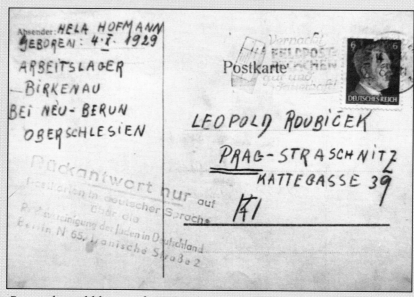

Postcards could be sent from Auschwitz to relatives abroad. However, by the time they had been censored in Berlin, their sender was almost certainly dead.

Striped uniform issued to prisoners at Auschwitz.

Blanket from Auschwitz, woven from a combination of used clothing and human hair.

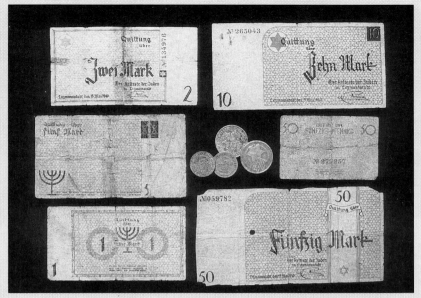

Ghetto money brought to Auschwitz by Jewish prisoners. Of course, there was nothing to buy in the camp, even had the owner survived long enough to spend the money.

The Nazis used a system of coloured stars sewn to prisoners' uniforms to identify national, political and religious groups. The word *Jude* against a yellow background indicated a Jew.

Crematorium ovens at Auschwitz–
Birkenau. Don Watt and his fellow
prisoners were forced to stoke the fires,
under the threat of being hurled into the
ovens themselves.

Name __WATT, D.J.__

File No.__ CO - 129398

QLD - 131003

DETERMINATION

The Committee determines that Mr Donald Joseph WATT is eligible to receive a non-taxable payment of $10,000.00 as compensation for having been illegally interned in a Nazi concentration camp during World War II and having been subjected to brutal treatment while in the Nazi concentration camp.

STATEMENT OF REASONS

The essential requirements as set by the Government for eligibility for compensation are that a veteran must have been interned illegally in a Nazi concentration camp, operated by a criminal Nazi organisation as defined by the Nuremburg War Crimes Tribunal, during World War II for a protracted period while being a member of the Australian Forces or an Australian in the Naval, Military or Air Forces of a Commonwealth or Allied country, and have suffered brutal treatment.

The Committee is satisfied that Mr Watt meets the eligibility criteria. He was an Australian veteran of World War II in that he served in the Australian Army. He was interned illegally in Auschwitz concentration camp. From Mr Watt's medical records it is obvious that he suffered brutal treatment while in the Nazi concentration camp. The Committee determines that Mr Watt is eligible for payment of a non-taxable lump sum of $10,000.00.

....
N. RALPH
(CHAIRMAN)

....
A.J. HILL
(MEMBER)

....
K. GRIMSLEY
(MEMBER)

17 April 1990

Official recognition at last of Don Watt's brutal treatment at the hands of the Nazis during his internment at Auschwitz–Birkenau.

the glory of being the man who made me talk. He was an absolute swine.

From what I can remember, they had plenty of customers at that Nuremberg centre. While I was in the cells, recovering after a beating, I could hear them working on other men who had been taken prisoner, pilots mainly, from the various Allied air forces. One was an American pilot who had been shot down. I could hear him screaming and under torture. I knew it wouldn't be long before he cracked, and it wasn't. Before long he was telling them which air base he had flown from, what his mission was, how many planes had come over, all that sort of thing. That's when it dawned on me: they already knew most of this information. They were just playing with the pilot, working him over for a bit of fun and seeing what else he could tell them that might be of use in the future.

The thing you have to understand is that the German intelligence system was so good they knew most of the information already. What their spies didn't tell them, they were able to pick up, one bit at a time, from the men they tortured. In this way, they soon knew everything there was to know about a particular mission and where different units were based. I was able to put all this together by listening through the walls to what was going on, and I thought, 'Right, you're not going to get me, you bastards.' They certainly tried, though.

For two days I was pistol-whipped, bashed about generally and punched all over the place. I told them I was an Australian, but for some reason they kept calling me an Englishman — 'stupid Englishman' and '*Englischer Schweinehund*', which I took to be 'English pig'. So far as they were concerned, if you spoke English, you were English, unless you were American, that is.

It soon became clear that there was no way a bashing was going to make me talk, so they lost patience with that routine and got out the thumbscrews — literally. With this major looking on, immaculate in his blue-grey uniform, they strapped my hand to a contraption on the table and proceeded to screw a clamp down over my thumb and then the fingers.

Taking one finger after another, they screwed down on them until the nail split. They kept this up for five or six days, until my hands could take it no more and my fingers and thumbs burst out at the ends. You know how sore your fingers and thumbs get when you trap them in a door or accidentally hit them with a hammer? Well, my fingers were like that. My hands were bloodied and red-raw, like two lumps of meat in a butcher's shop. And so sore.

On the seventh day, I could tell the major was beginning to lose patience, or what little patience he had. He was becoming more and more irrational. He'd start screaming at me for no reason at all, his lips going white at the corners of his mouth. He was one of those men you can look at and know instantly that they're a right bastard. He was a tallish, thin-faced, thin-lipped man. You could tell from his expression that he didn't do much laughing. I reckon he could have sat through ten Marx Brothers movies and not cracked a single smile. Then, without a word, he slowly took out his Nazi dagger, one with a swastika on the handle. Looking me straight in the eye, he chopped the tip off the middle finger of my left hand. It hurt so much I nearly cracked. With blood going everywhere, I called him all the names under the sun, all the dirty so-and-sos, all the rotten stinking bastards I could think of. This was a total reflex action on my part and was quite stupid, as it only made him madder. At one stage he even took out his gun, held it to my temple and cocked the hammer. I thought he was going to blow my brains out, but he put the gun away and bashed me around some more, keeping it up until I collapsed on the floor.

I woke up next morning on the floor of a cell, aching in every bone of my body. An orderly came in, wiped the blood off my face and gave me a hunk of bread and some water. My hands were so raw that I could hardly hold the bread or the cup and, thirsty as I was, my lips were so swollen, bloodied and cracked that it was all I could do just to sip. An hour or so later, the major came in again, tall and arrogant in jodhpur trousers and polished boots that came up to his knees, and a peaked cap with the outstretched eagle on it. He seemed a bit calmer this time. He put the same questions to me again: 'How did you get your clothes?' 'Where did you get your money?' 'How did you get your papers?' I just kept telling him the same story, 'I'm Corporal Donald Watt of the Australian Army. My serial number is VX8006. I am a prisoner of war. My POW number is 10418 and I have escaped from Stalag 357 in Poland.'

'All right, you stupid Englishman' he said. 'All right, you *Englischer Schweinehund*. You won't talk, yes? You don't like to talk? Well, that is good. That is fine. If you do not want to talk, I will send you to a place where you won't have to talk. You will go to Auschwitz. For a year. We will see how you like talking then.'

CHAPTER 6
Auschwitz

Next day I was taken under guard to the railway station, where I was bundled onto a train. We travelled till late afternoon, when we were forced to stop because Allied planes had come over during the night and bombed large sections of road and the railway line. There was chaos everywhere. Roads were broken up, railway services in chaos, men in uniform running all over the place, everyone shouting orders, and no-one doing very much about it. To me this was good news, brilliant news, but I didn't think I should tell my guard what I thought. He didn't seem the type to appreciate any sort of a joke, let alone one at the expense of the Reich.

Determined to press on, the guard commandeered a truck from somewhere and we went by road to another railway line, where I was locked up overnight in a German army barracks. The next morning, around 7 a.m., I was bundled onto another train for what seemed an interminable journey, hours upon hours of stopping and starting, while the American Air Force increased its daylight raids. I could hear the Flying Fortresses overhead, and the awesome 'kerrump, kerrump' as bombs rained down on roads, railways, bridges, tunnels and all manner of other strategic targets. Around noon we pulled into a small station in the middle of nowhere — we were at the end of the line. Word went around that the line up ahead was damaged beyond immediate repair and, along with everyone else, I was off-loaded and left standing around, waiting for alternative transport. I must say my guard was resourceful — or was in a unit that didn't take no for an answer — because in no time at all he had commandeered a large panel van, and we were on the road again.

I think the guard must have panicked at this point. With all the bombing that was taking place, I think he lost his nerve a little and decided to take the easy way out, heading for what he guessed would be safe territory. After driving hell-for-leather for several hours, we arrived at a camp called Belsen, where I was to stay for eight days. Long after the war, I was able to look at an atlas and was amazed how far north we had gone. We were supposed to be going east into southern Poland, but here we were near a village called Bergen, in the middle of Luneburg Heath in northern Germany.

We pulled up at the gates and the guard let me out of the back door of the van. 'Belsen,' he said, nodding his head towards the main gate. That was the only time, and the only word, he spoke during the whole journey from Nuremberg. I stood there while he presented his papers to the guards on the gate. Dusk was falling, but I could clearly see the grim-faced guards dressed in dark-green uniforms and carrying submachine guns, and the usual barbed-wire fences stretching on both sides as far as the eye could see. While one guard pointed his machine gun straight at us, another checked our papers and waved us through, pointing to what I assumed was one of the administration huts.

While all this was going on, I was trying to get my bearings. I tried to work out how long we had been travelling and in which direction, but just as my mind was grappling with the subject, my nose was sending me another, quite different message. There was a smell, a strange smell that rekindled memories of my youth around Mildura. I noticed the smell the moment we arrived at Belsen, but somehow I pushed it to the back of my mind. Then the smell was in my nostrils again, insistent, demanding attention, a smell that caught at the back of my throat and made me want to gag. I then recognised it for what it was. With my mind going back to the lush fields of Mildura, I remembered the times I had come across a cow or a sheep that had strayed out of a paddock and been hit by a car or truck. By the time I came upon the carcass, it was usually rotting away in an advanced state of decay. And that's what I could smell around Belsen: the smell of death. Even my guard looked uneasy.

With a guard watching over me all the time, I was locked in an office for an hour or so and then marched off to a large wooden shed that housed between 50 and 60 men, sitting, lying and, in some cases, sleeping on the floor. There were no chairs, no beds, no bunks. The men were thin, pathetic-looking people, wearing the coarse, blue-grey striped shirt and pants that I now know was the standard uniform for concentration-camp prisoners throughout the Third Reich. They looked at me without interest. I was just another face, another body, and it was clear they had seen plenty come and go. I was nothing to them.

These men weren't the walking skeletons that I was soon to come across at Auschwitz, but it is also very clear that they had been without medical attention and living on starvation rations for a very long time. I had been trying to keep my spirits up since my arrest near the Swiss border, but now, for the first time, I was starting to feel really depressed. I was missing the comradeship of my mates, and the future wasn't looking good. Suddenly, I needed to go to the toilet and I indicated this in sign language to one of the prisoners. He pointed to a large metal bin outside the hut. Privacy? Forget it. There wasn't any.

Although the hut I was assigned to was crowded when I arrived, the number of men in it soon grew to around 200. We were just jammed in together, making it impossible to sit or lie down without having someone else's body hard up against you. The stink was terrible: a rank mixture of stale body odour and human excrement. It was as though they hadn't showered or washed for months. Some of them were lousy, too, spending hours on end running their hands and fingers over their bodies and through their hair, catching lice and other bugs and crushing them between their fingernails. Others didn't bother about the bugs. Sometimes I would see lice crawling through their hair, while they merely sat there, doing nothing about it. My skin crawled just looking at them.

Health seemed to be a major problem. With all the lice, bugs, fleas, dirt and excrement, I wasn't surprised when I heard from some of the inmates that typhus was a major scourge at Belsen. Some men would lie on the ground at night, moaning deliriously and so weak they were unable to move. Others had persistent coughs, which I took to be a sign of tuberculosis. I was feeling really flat. 'This is it, Don, m'boy,' I thought. 'If the Nazi bastards don't get you, some bloody disease will!'

Every second day, or just when the number of men in the hut grew so large that it was almost impossible to breathe, we were ordered to line up on the parade ground. Once we had lined up — just a couple of huts, 400 or so men at a time — the guards came along and picked people out, seemingly at random, but always the weakest. I thought they were being picked because they needed urgent medical attention, but the official line was that they were being sent to neighbouring farms, where they would work for their keep. I soon realised this was a monstrous lie.

Possibly because I was only in transit, and wearing a French army uniform instead of prison gear, I wasn't hassled as much as the other prisoners and was allowed to walk a few yards from my hut. I don't mean I was able to go for great long walks, but I was able to sticky-beak a bit. What I saw appalled me. I was walking near the perimeter fence one day, when I saw a Russian work party digging big trenches and throwing dead bodies in. Most of the bodies were naked, but some were still wearing prison shirts with yellow triangles on them, showing they were Jews. That's when the penny dropped: these were the very people who had been told they were going to work on farms, and they had marched off, uncomplaining, straight to their deaths. Now they were being buried in mass graves, their bodies lazily thrown into a monstrous hole in the ground.

That perimeter fence was quite educational. Not only did I see mass graves being dug, but also what appeared to be piles of dark clothing stacked right up against the fence at different intervals. However, you didn't need to get too close to these 'bundles' to realise they were dead bodies, the rotting corpses of poor demented souls who had been shot down for running or walking up to the fence. The bodies, rotting and festering, had been left there by the guards and the camp administration as a deterrent to others.

I don't know what sort of treatment I expected to receive in this camp, whether I had a privileged status as a POW or had been marked down for brutal treatment because of my refusal to talk back at Nuremberg, but after seeing bodies being thrown into mass graves, those line-ups bloody scared me. At the next one, the SS guards stopped selecting victims just two prisoners away from me, and I broke out into a trembling sweat. 'Jesus!' I thought. 'Is that what's going to happen to me?'

Feeling absolutely certain that I was going to be picked out for something, I made a point of never standing in the same place twice. I hopped from one line to another and from one end of a line to another, trying to get to a position I thought would be safe. At the next line-up, they stopped picking at the man standing next to me, and at the one after that they picked out the men standing on either side of me, leaving me sweating and trembling and feeling sick to the stomach. I really thought my number was up.

I know Belsen was a concentration camp, where tens of thousands of people perished (mainly from disease and malnutrition) from the middle of 1944 to April 1945, but during the eight days I was there towards the end of April 1944, it seemed more like a transit and detention camp. Most of the prisoners seemed to be Jews, who were being locked up until they could be sent to other countries, such as Palestine, in exchange for German civilians interned in Britain, Canada or the United States.

New arrivals came in every day, train and truckloads of them, many exhausted and worn out from working in slave-labour factories. As they came in, similar numbers of prisoners left the camp, going, I heard, to the factories of the Ruhr Valley. Other prisoners were simply being transported to the gas chambers of Auschwitz. The first time I heard this, my insides turned to water. Until then, I hadn't known the first thing about Auschwitz. To me it was just a name, another camp, although somewhat tougher than the POW camps I was used to. Now, however, it was starting to dawn on me: I was being sent to a death camp.

The journey to Auschwitz took two days. As soon we arrived and my papers had been processed, I was taken to an underground cell block and placed in a cell by myself. I don't know how many cells there were, but they were all occupied, mainly by Poles. I was the only English-speaking person. We lived in complete darkness, not knowing what time of day it was or whether it was day or night. The only time there was the faintest glimmer of light was when the guards opened an outside door, came along with a torch and dropped a small piece of bread and a cup of water through the steel bars. Occasionally, if we were very lucky, there would be a small piece of blood sausage or a lump of cheese. But you had to be quick. The first day I was there, I completely missed out on a meal. I wasn't sure what was happening and before I realised food had been distributed, rats had got to the bread and cheese.

That night the other people in the cells started talking to me. They were Poles who spoke German and knew a bit of English so, with the bit of German I had picked up, I was able to make myself understood. I told them I was Australian, an Aussie, which they pronounced 'Aw-sie' or 'Os-sie', and they explained the routine to me: when the food arrived, where the toilet bin was, that sort of thing.

Next day, when the meagre rations were issued, I was quicker, and threw myself on top of the food as soon as it was thrown through the bars. Trouble was, my fingers were still so sore and swollen from the torture sessions at Nuremberg that it was hard for me to pick the food off the ground. I had to hold the scraps in the heels of my hands as best I could. Added to that, my face was so swollen from the beating I had taken I could only nibble small pieces at a time. At least my food lasted longer this way, and I had all day to eat it.

The men in the other cells were intrigued that I was an Australian and wanted to know what I had done to be in Auschwitz. When I told them I had escaped from a POW camp, they wanted to know why I hadn't been shot. I didn't have an answer to that. They explained that they were in the cells for giving cheek to the guards or answering back, or for being trouble-makers. When I asked them why they hadn't been shot, they had no answer, either.

I'll never forget those underground cells. They were roughly 1.25 metres wide by 2.25 metres long (four feet by seven feet six inches), with brick walls at the back and sides. The front was a full-length iron grill, with thick steel bars ten centimetres (four inches) apart. The door was on the left. Feeling my way around in the dark, I found the toilet bin at the front, three bars in from the right-hand wall. For some reason, the bin was outside the grill, making it very hard to use, and, of course, there was no paper or water for the prisoners to clean themselves. The stench from the bins, the stink of the rats, and our own body odour combined to make the smell in the cells unbelievable. Living in these conditions, many prisoners died of dysentery, suffering a terrible ordeal.

The worst thing about the cells was the rats. Not only did you have to make sure they didn't get your food, you had to watch out that they didn't get you. The first night I was there, the man in the cell next to me started singing in a fairly loud voice, and a few others joined in. I didn't know what was going on. They explained later that this was the system they had devised to keep the rats away while one or two people slept or dozed. If everyone slept at the same time, leaving the cells totally quiet, the rats would move in and start to eat the first person they came across. I shivered when they told me that. As a result, we slept in relays, two or three at a time, with the others singing away or talking loudly to keep the rats out.

At the beginning, I tried to keep the rats at bay by catching a few and breaking their necks, the way I killed rabbits back home. I'd grab a rat, hold its head on the ground with my foot and then pull it up sharply by the back legs. When I heard the neck crack, I'd chuck the dead body through the bars for the other rats to eat. I thought this was a good idea, until the man in the next cell asked me what the squealing was. When I explained, he warned me not to do it again. He said that rats were intelligent animals, that they would quickly work out where the food was coming from, and would wait for me to throw them a feed. If I failed, the chances were they would attack me — literally biting the hand (or any other part of the body) that fed them.

For some pathetic prisoners in the underground cells, there was no escaping the rats. Those who were too ill or feeble to fend for themselves were attacked regularly. I would sit there in the dark, listening to their pitiful cries, while they were eaten alive. After a couple of days, when the feeding frenzy had ended, the guards would open the door, take out what was left of the bodies and the rotting clothes, and throw a new prisoner in.

I was in the underground cell for what I reckoned must have been seven or eight weeks. Because of the darkness, I wasn't able to make any marks on the wall and lost track of time, so I'm only guessing here. It was during this time that I realised how I'd managed to escape the gas chamber at Belsen. I thought I'd been smart in moving to different positions in different lines, but I now realised that the SS had been using me as a marker. I'd been wearing a French uniform since my civilian clothes were taken from me back at Nuremberg, and the Germans had known I was an Australian. The way I'd dodged around to avoid being picked! That made me laugh, right out loud in the dark.

In the next cell, one of the Poles said, in German, 'Os-sie is going mad!' It's surprising how much of the language I had picked up, but I'd been a POW for more than three years by then, and you learn fast when you are being shouted at in German and get clouted with a rifle butt if you don't jump smartly. My laughing made the other prisoners wonder what was up. When I explained, they all laughed, too. It was like that in all my seven months at Auschwitz: you would seize on the smallest thing and make a joke out of it. Anything for a laugh, I suppose.

Eventually, after an eternity in the cells, I was dragged out into the daylight. The sun seared my eyes, and I tried to put a hand up to shield them from the glare. For this I was rewarded with a clout from a rifle butt and a snarl to keep moving. I was taken to a storeroom, given a long, striped, concentration camp shirt, and then led to a large wooden hut, where 40 or 50 men lived. I soon learnt that they had been taken prisoner for various 'offences.' Some were political prisoners, others were Jews, but most were Poles — all of them identified by coloured triangles on their shirts.

Efficient at everything, including the classification of human beings, the Nazis had devised an identification system for everyone in the camp, based on coloured cloth triangles. Jews wore a yellow triangle, political prisoners red. A yellow and red Star of David was for Jews imprisoned for political activities or for being married to a non-Jew. There were other triangles: the Capos, the dreaded camp foremen, wore green (the triangle for common criminals); black was for social outcasts, such as work evaders and prostitutes; pink for homosexuals; brown for gypsies; purple for Catholic priests and monks; and violet for Jehovah's Witnesses.

At first the SS guards didn't know what to do with me. I wasn't a political prisoner, I wasn't a Jew or a gypsy, a homosexual or a communist, and I wasn't Russian or Polish. I defied categorisation, and I think this offended their German sense of order. So, for the first two nights after being released from the underground cell, I was placed in a hut with a mixture of prisoners, some political, some Jews. After that I was transferred to another wooden hut containing about 100 men, all Polish. Their crime seemed to be just that: being Polish. To me, however, they seemed decent enough people, who were most intrigued that they had a genuine prisoner of war in their midst, and an Australian at that.

Using the bit of German I had picked up, I learnt that the Poles worked as stokers. By this time, what with my experience at Belsen, I had a fair idea of what the furnaces were used for, but my mind still hadn't come to grips with the full impact of what was taking place. I had heard that mass murder — outright genocide — was taking place. But was this really true? Could I believe it? It seemed impossible. It defied comprehension. But the answer is yes, it was true. When I asked the Poles what they burnt in the furnaces, there was a silence, and then, eventually, one of them said, *'Juden'* — Jews. Next morning I joined them, walking the 100 metres (300 feet) or so to the crematoria, where we spent the entire day throwing logs in to keep the fires going, while other men working alongside me threw dead bodies in. Even now, 50 years later, it sickens me just to think of it.

I soon learnt that I was in Auschwitz–Birkenau, or Auschwitz II, part of a massive concentration-camp complex at Oswiecim, near Krakow in southern Poland, which included Auschwitz I and Auschwitz–Monowice, also known as Auschwitz III. Auschwitz–Birkenau was the death camp, the extermination camp where the mass killings took place. And the deaths occurred there on such a mammoth scale, with such awesomely unfailing regularity, that I could have been on a production line.

It worked like this. Cattle trains with trucks loaded with people marked for death pulled up right inside the camp. The doors were opened and the people ordered to get down and line up. Some were selected for work camps or medical experiments, while the rest, the vast majority, were marched over to the gas chambers, hundreds at a time. They were told they were about to be deloused and given a shower, and had to strip. After the shower, they were told, they would be given camp clothing and assigned to work parties.

As the world now knows, this was nothing but lies, lies, lies. There was no shower, there was no food, there was no special clothing. Instead, they were locked in the gas chamber

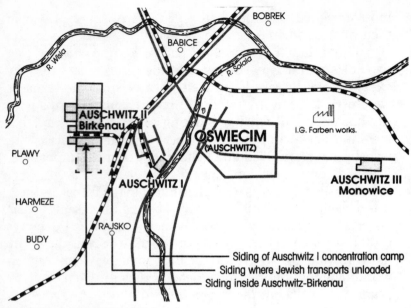

Auschwitz concentration camp

and gas pellets thrown in. After 20 minutes, they were dead. The doors were then opened and the bodies pulled out. Their hair was cut off, their mouths inspected for gold teeth, which were ripped out with pincers, and their fingers checked for rings. Their bodies were then trundled over to the crematorium, where they were thrown into the furnace. Gangs of men, just like me, kept the fires burning brightly. I was told you could smell burning human flesh up to 25 kilometres (15 miles) away.

Gas was one thing they had in plenty — that, and people to use it on. The deadly Zyklon B gas, with its cyanide base, was made by the Degesch company, and vast quantities were delivered at the height of the gassings. I know, because I saw the drums. At first there was a rumour that the gas was being made at the I. G. Farben chemical works at nearby Monowice — a plant built by Jewish slave labour — and there was talk of getting word to the Americans or the RAF so they could bomb the place. We later heard that it was only an oil and synthetic-rubber plant.

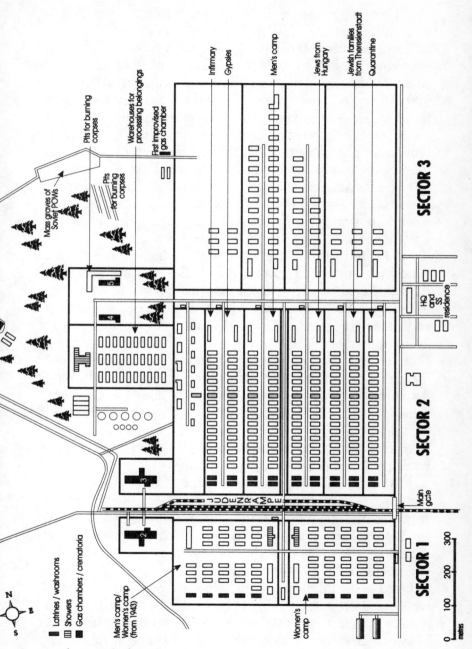

Auschwitz II (Birkenau)

I worked mainly with Polish men from my hut, and it was a case of either do the despicable job as the SS guards ordered, or suffer a terrible fate. The work was hard, physical and remorseless, and some buckled and collapsed under the strain. Within three months of working at the furnace, I saw 100 of my co-workers die — some from malnutrition, some from disease, some from mental breakdowns which reduced them to shaking wrecks, and some from sheer exhaustion. Others simply gave up. Whatever the reason for their death, their bodies were disposed of in the same way — straight into the furnace. This was Auschwitz–Birkenau, and there was no place for the sick or the weak. Those who could not work were simply thrown into the furnace. I know. I saw it. I was there.

The four gas chambers and four crematoria at Birkenau were kept busy right around the clock. Holidays and Sundays didn't exist in those death factories. Every day, trainloads of Jewish men, women and children, gypsies, communists and other 'undesirables' arrived at the camp, sometimes at 90-minute intervals. By counting the bodies as they trundled over to the furnaces, I estimated that from May 1944 until the end of November 1944, Crematorium 2 and Crematorium 3 each disposed of 5000 corpses every 24 hours, seven days a week. I can't speak for the other two gas chamber-crematoria complexes, numbers 1 and 4, because I didn't work at them. I did hear, however, that they were somewhat smaller than numbers 2 and 3, and had less capacity.

At times during my seven months at Auschwitz, particularly around July and August of 1944, there were so many gassings taking place that the crematoria couldn't keep up. But the Nazis had provided for even this sick eventuality. Whenever the trains brought in so many people that the gas chambers and crematoria couldn't cope, gassing time was reduced to ten minutes and, to help with the disposal, bodies were burnt on pyres. Pyres had been used in the early days at Auschwitz, and the sites were still there. Thick layers of brushwood were placed on the ground and one or two layers of bodies placed on top, Then came more brushwood and more bodies, up to a height of a couple of metres, maybe more. Fuel was poured over them and the whole thing set alight. It was monstrous work — not that I had to do it — but from the bored, unconcerned, unemotional look on the faces of the guards, you would think they were supervising a backyard burn-off.

We lived in the most unbelievable conditions. Most of us were troubled by lice, which laid eggs in the seams of our clothes, and we scratched ourselves all night long. Every now and again I was able to scrounge an extra shirt which I turned into a pair of underpants by tying the sleeves around my waist. I kept the other shirt near the furnace so the heat would kill the eggs, and changed shirts as often as possible. The rest of our clothing was basic, even primitive. We had no socks and wore wooden clogs instead of shoes. Most of the time, however, I worked barefoot. You could work faster that way, and this saved you from being called lazy and being beaten up by the guards.

These same guards also got into the habit of stealing our food, such as it was. Because of the war, Germany and Poland were going through terrible food shortages, and the guards were regularly in our kitchens, helping themselves to our soup and bread — there was no way that they were going to go hungry. Because of the food situation, malnutrition among the prisoners grew steadily worse, resulting in hundreds more dying. And all the time, the SS guards screamed at us to work harder, work harder.

But no matter how badly we were treated, how brutal the guards, how poor the food, how bad the lice, how stinking the conditions, the Russian prisoners seemed to have it worse, probably because of the huge losses their troops inflicted on the Germans on the Russian front and at the siege of Stalingrad. At Auschwitz, whenever there were any really dirty, hard or menial jobs to be done, it was always the Russian prisoners who did them.

The other prisoners with the really rotten jobs were

the people conscripted into the special squads, or *Sonder-kommando*. They had to remove the bodies from the gas chambers, cut off the hair, pull out the gold teeth and throw the corpses into the furnaces. They were chosen chiefly from among Jewish prisoners of the nationalities currently arriving at the camp. Their numbers varied, depending on the size of the truck convoys and cattle trains arriving at Birkenau, and they were housed separately from the rest of the prisoners, in quarters near the crematoria.

It must have been hideous, heartbreaking, brutalising work, pulling the teeth and burning the bodies of people who had died for no other reason than their beliefs or nationality, but those who objected were killed on the spot. In July 1944, a couple of months after I arrived, nearly 450 young Greek Jews were gassed for refusing to work on the *Sonderkommando*. This sent a grim message to everyone else.

The *Sonderkommando* also had the task of cleaning the crematoria, shovelling out the ashes and taking them away to be buried or scattered throughout the surrounding countryside. You might think that all this ash would have made good fertiliser, but in the quantities Birkenau was producing every day, it was simply toxic. Apart from the forested areas, the land surrounding the camp became more like a lunar landscape by the day, a scene of utter desolation, where nothing would grow.

My job, stoking the fires, was despicable work, and I knew it. However, three of us, myself and two good Polish men I worked with for quite a while, decided to take no notice of what was happening around us and just keep working, stoking, and trying to stay alive. The mental strain was incredible, always having to say and do the right thing so we didn't anger the guards and get on the wrong end of a belting. We sometimes asked ourselves whether it was worth it. Day after day, we wondered if we would ever be free, or would we just carry on, stoking the furnaces until we dropped? And what if we didn't drop? Chances were the guards would kill us anyway, just so there would be no witnesses to the cold-blooded mass murder that was taking place.

You have to understand that the Germans who ran the camps, the Waffen SS and the Capos, were extremely callous men, the worst kind of sadists. They were absolute bastards, every one of them. Nothing was abhorrent to them, nothing too unspeakable. You never knew from one day to the next what fiendish, sickening act of brutality they would come up with. We knew this, we all knew this, and we kept our heads down. Any sign from any of us that we were refusing to do their dreadful work would have led to our instant deaths. I mean this quite literally. The guards thought nothing of killing people, even for sport.

From time to time, just for the hell of it, they would pick out one of the weakest workers and cut off his penis with a bayonet or knife. Other workers were disembowelled. The men would cry out in agony, and their mates would then rush over to see what was happening. This is what the guards wanted. They would aim their rifles at the men who rushed over, shoot them in the legs and then have them thrown into the furnaces alive. They did this for the sheer pleasure of hearing the men scream. They actually stood around, smiling, laughed and joking about it. It was sickening to see human beings behave in this way. Whenever it happened, the other workers would be so frightened that they would work even harder. For some, this proved fatal. Barely having enough strength and energy to support themselves, let alone work harder, they collapsed through exhaustion.

I think most of us considered suicide at some time in Auschwitz. What kept us going was the knowledge that, despite the barbarity of what was going on around us, life really was precious. We were also spurred on by the hope that, although we were living a nightmare, it would end one day, and we would be released from this death camp. Some prisoners who couldn't stand the mental torment found a way of killing themselves by throwing themselves onto the electrified fence that surrounded the camp. Some even ran headlong into it. You could hear them screaming as the current went through them, snatching their life away. A few of us tried to stop them committing suicide, but they pushed us away angrily, saying it was better to go that way than in the gas chamber, or be thrown alive into the furnace. The Nazis didn't care either way. When we went to retrieve the bodies, the guards told us to let them rot where they were, as a deterrent to others.

There was one activity that took place at Auschwitz that now, 50 years later, makes me wonder about the Germans' hatred of Jews. Oh, they hated them all right, but they didn't mind using them as a human blood bank so that German soldiers could live. It happened like this: in the women's camp next to us, 600 or 700 of the healthiest Jewish women were specially selected by the SS and placed in cages along the walls of a large hut. The SS then went along to each cage with big syringes and removed blood from the women.

They kept it up, day after day, until the women were too weak or too sick to give any more blood. When that happened, they were taken to the gas chambers and a fresh lot of women put into the cages. I have to say that I didn't see this particular activity taking place, but I heard about it from other prisoners. And I certainly saw the corpses, with their arms and bodies covered in puncture marks. I sometimes wonder what the German soldiers in the field hospitals would have thought if they'd known they were receiving Jewish blood.

The Jews at Auschwitz were rarely able to strike back, but there are some people whose spirit you can't break. Even in a hellish place like Auschwitz, there was resistance, insurrection and rebellion. One uprising that took place while I was there involved some of the women prisoners and the *Sonderkommando*.

The *Sonderkommando*, the people used for the most disgusting work, were the biggest threat to the SS. They had the potential to denounce the SS guards' wanton barbarism. They had seen the worst of the atrocities, and if the Allies gained the upper hand in the war and trials for war crimes took place, they would make star witnesses for the prosecution. Naturally, therefore, the SS wanted them disposed of, and word came from the SS High Command that the *Sonderkommando* were to be liquidated every few months. For their part, the *Sonderkommando* knew they were living on borrowed time. They knew there was no way the SS would let them live, so they set about preparing an uprising. The numerous women prisoners who worked in the nearby Union explosives factory played a central role by smuggling dynamite into the camp.

Having increased to 1000 at the height of the Birkenau exterminations, the size of the *Sonderkommando* had decreased to 200 by the late summer of 1944, when it was decided to liquidate them gradually. Fourteen were sent to the main Auschwitz camp for gassing. However, when this leaked out on the underground network, the remaining members of the *Sonderkommando* prepared to hit back. When the guards went over to Crematorium 3 to round up the next batch of 14, a riot broke out. The *Sonderkommando* attacked the guards, taking them completely by surprise. They seized their rifles and opened fire, killing three SS officers and wounding others. With the dynamite already in place, they lit the fuse and blew up the crematorium, starting a huge fire which destroyed the furnace and put it out of action for good.

I was working on Crematorium 2 at the time, and the blast took us all by surprise. The explosion was so loud, so severe, that whole bricks went flying through the air and the ground shook under our feet. At first we thought we'd been caught in a bombing raid (there had been talk over the months of getting a message to the Allies about what was going on at Auschwitz), but we hadn't heard any planes overhead and there had been no air-raid warning.

There was instant pandemonium. Everyone stopped what they were doing, even the guards, and rushed to have a look. Smoke and brick dust filled the air, and we all felt quite disoriented. What had happened? What had gone wrong? Some sort of malfunction? Don't tell me — no, it's impossible — don't tell me someone had actually hit back! Once they were over the initial shock, the guards panicked and opened fire on the huge crowd that had formed. Realising almost instantly that this was some sort of revolt, they rushed over from every part of the camp, submachine guns at the ready, and started firing at random, spraying bullets everywhere. It was a shooting gallery. Before long, hundreds of dead and wounded bodies were lying all over the place. It was then that I realised how lucky I'd been. I'd just spent a month working on Crematorium 3 and had been back at Number 2 for only a couple of weeks. If the uprising had been much earlier, it's London to a brick that I'd have been killed along with the others, if not in the explosion, then certainly in the brutal retaliation that followed.

As it was, all of us on the furnaces and the gas chambers were forced to work even harder, to get more people gassed and more bodies burnt. Crematorium 3, like Crematorium 2, was a high-capacity furnace. With the guards yelling and screaming at us to work harder and go faster, it was up to us to make sure their 'production figures' didn't take too much of a dip.

The brave act of resistance and sabotage in knocking out Crematorium 3 saved roughly 5000 lives a day, but it came at a price, with more than 400 prisoners being killed in the rebellion or murdered in retaliation. Those who used the uprising to escape from the camp were hunted down and shot. Almost immediately, camp informants, keen to ingratiate themselves with the hierarchy, told the SS they had heard rumours about women prisoners smuggling gunpowder into the camp. The SS responded by planting dozens of women spies to work undercover to see who was responsible.

I'm not sure if they found who was directly responsible for the explosives, but they did turn up one Jewish woman who had been smuggling messages to her brother in another part of Auschwitz, using as an intermediary one of the SS guards who seemed to have a bit of decency in him. They arrested the woman and three of her friends and tortured them for days on end. God alone knows what sort of torments they must have gone through but, at the end, they were taken out and hanged, their bodies left to dangle and rot on the gallows as a lasting reminder for all to see.

To me, the entire incident was utterly heroic. With the odds stacked heavily against them, and death and destruction confronting them every day, at least some of the prisoners of Auschwitz had showed that they were not prepared to give in without a fight, no matter how futile. They showed they weren't just victims and passive witnesses, but also fearless opponents of Nazism. And the way the women, in particular, underwent the most brutal interrogation without cracking is an eloquent lesson in humanity for us all.

CHAPTER 7
A Typical Day

Life in Auschwitz proceeded according to a routine that was so strict, so regular, that you could set your watch by it. From the moment we were kicked awake at 5.30 a.m., until we were back in our barracks at around 6.30 p.m., we were watched every minute of the day. We also had to work hard, very hard. Any slacking was rewarded with the thump of a rifle butt in the back if we were lucky, and if we weren't lucky . . . well, more of that later.

We would be woken by the Capos, the loathed, feared 'foremen' of Auschwitz who pretty well ran the camp on behalf of the Waffen SS. The Capos performed other duties as well, for which they were rewarded with extra food, when it was available, and visits to the camp brothel. The Capos were common criminals — rapists, murderers, armed robbers — the scum of the jails. They were sadistic bastards, every one of them, who couldn't believe their luck at being put in charge of people who mattered even less than they did. And they loved their work.

' *'Raus, 'raus. Mach' schnell,*' they would yell, waking us with a kick in the back or a boot in the groin as we lay sleeping on the ground. It was their job to bully us into a state of cowering servility. They were on constant lookout for any sign of rebellion or resistance, and the more prisoners they could dob into the guards for surliness or for not working hard, the better they looked, the greater their rewards and the more they revelled in their grotesque power. They were thugs who wore their brutality like a badge of honour, and at times they performed acts far more horrendous than those of the SS guards.

Once awake, we received a scrap of bread and maybe a bit of cheese or sausage for breakfast. Then, with no time to go to the toilet block, we trudged off to work to carry out the various chores we had been assigned. And all the chores, no matter what they were, were directed towards a single end — the mass destruction of human life.

Wearing nothing but a striped prison camp shirt, we arrived at the furnaces at six. They had been cleaned out during the night, all the ashes of the previous day shovelled away, and a small fire left burning inside. Then, working in gangs of three, we threw wood onto the fire and built up the blaze. I worked mainly at Crematorium 2 and sometimes at Crematorium 3. There were four crematoria at Auschwitz–Birkenau. Numbers 2 and 3 were identical, standing about 1.3 metres (roughly seven feet) high on either side of the railway line that carried the death trains into the camp. The furnaces were built of brick and reinforced concrete, with a convex roof that was able to withstand massive heat, and the subsequent expansion and contraction, without cracking. I was told that the other two crematoria, numbers 1 and 4, were on the other side of the camp, just across from a group of warehouses containing the personal effects of the murdered victims. However, I didn't ever see them.

We worked at the side of the crematorium, where there were five three-door furnaces with two generator hearths in each. The bottom doors were about 60 centimetres (two feet) off the ground. We fed the wood through these and onto a grate that looked as though it was made from cast-iron bars. The wood came in from the forest of fir trees to the northwest of the camp, on large, high-sided wagons about 3.5 metres by 2 metres (12 feet by six) that were pushed and pulled along by a dozen Russian prisoners. The wood was then stacked into a huge pile, located centrally to the crematoria.

Other gangs would then load smaller wagons at this central wood pile and bring it over to the furnaces, heaping it into four smaller piles, one pile between each set of triple doors, so wood could be fed into the furnace from either side.

Starting from scratch, moving from one stoking-hole to another, it would take us about 20 minutes to have the furnaces roaring. That's when the first bodies of the day would arrive. As I write these words, I feel sick to the stomach at the memory of it all. As I said earlier, my experience at Belsen and the few words I'd had with the Poles in my hut had given me no doubt about what was being burnt in the furnaces. However, nothing had prepared me for the sight of the bodies as they were trundled over to the furnace from the gas chamber, piled high on an open-sided cart, 80, 90, 100 at a time. Completely naked, the bodies were smeared with vomit and excrement, their hair cut short, and eyes wide open and staring maniacally. Their mouths were agape, locked open in the shriek of fear that would have gripped them amidst the stark realisation that they had been cheated to the end and were now being gassed to death.

The gas chambers at Birkenau were actually underground, on the western side of the camp, about 50 to 100 metres (150 to 300 feet) in from the perimeter fence. The trains, with their pitiful cargo of unwanted humanity, would come to a halt alongside a platform, or ramp, towards the southern side of the camp between crematoria 2 and 3. One by one, the cattle trucks would open and the bewildered, wretched people inside — 100 to a truck — would be ordered down onto the platform to line up, and a selection process would begin, conducted by doctors, nurses and senior Waffen SS officers.

Strong people who could work were drafted into the Auschwitz work gangs. Pretty girls and young women went to the brothels for the sexual pleasure of the SS guards and selected Capos. Others were chosen for medical experiments, while the remainder — the old and the sick, babies, pregnant women and women with children — were marked for instant destruction.

In an unending stream, they were marched under SS guard to the gas chamber courtyard, where they were ordered to strip before being crammed into what they thought was a bath-house, hundreds upon hundreds at a time. Once the doors had been locked and barred to make escape impossible, the gas was introduced through a special opening. I heard from my new workmates that carbon monoxide had earlier been the killer gas, but some months before my arrival they had changed to Zyklon B, which was administered in pellet form. The pellets, small pieces of diatomite, were soaked or heavily impregnated with Zyklon B and stored in small drums. They gave off deadly fumes the instant they were released to the air.

It was fairly common for the people locked in the bath-house to notice, in the handful of seconds, perhaps half a minute, before the gas was released, that the shower heads were phoney and to scream with the realisation of what was about to happen. The moment this occurred, the moment they started to breathe in the gas, a truck kept nearby would start up and noisily rev its engine to drown out their cries, which only lasted a couple of minutes. After 20 minutes, when the people were dead and the gas had evaporated, the *Sonderkommando* went in to drag out the bodies, cut the hair, inspect the corpses for rings and gold teeth, and pile them onto wagons to be wheeled over to the crematoria. And so it went on, with trainload after trainload of innocent people, thousands upon thousands of them, coming into Auschwitz–Birkenau, and exterminations taking place around the clock.

Working in concert with this production line of death were scores of other prisoners whose job it was to collect the piles of discarded clothing and other possessions, and wheel them in handcarts over to a warehouse for sorting. Clothes went into one heap, shoes into another, children's toys into a third. I was told that the clothes were collected and distributed to loyal Germans throughout the Reich. Often the warehouses were so full that belongings were piled up alongside the ramp and left outside the warehouse for days on end.

I have no way of knowing what went through the minds

of any prisoners still standing on the platform, but it would have been pointless for them to try to escape. As soon as they were off-loaded from the trains, all approach and transit roads were cleared and closed, and it was strictly forbidden for other prisoners to go near the latest arrivals.

The bodies had a curious pink tinge to them when they arrived at the crematorium, caused, I imagine, by a chemical reaction with the gas. Often, they still had the stink of the gas on them. It's a smell I'll never forget, although it's hard to describe — perhaps a touch of sulphur and bad eggs. It was so long ago and, at the time, we weren't able to stand around and discuss it too much. There was also the smell of the burning bodies, a sickly smell that invaded your nose, throat and every pore of your body, making you want to retch. It's a smell that has stayed with me through the years, but how to describe it? In my years of working on different farms, I got to know and recognise the smell of cattle and sheep burning. It wasn't a pleasant smell, but all I can say is that the smell of human bodies burning was infinitely worse. It was a smell that took months, nearly a year, to pass from my system — such a horrible smell, that it makes me gag even to think about it.

And if the look of horror on the faces of the bodies wasn't enough, there was worse to come. The bodies of children were often buried among the adults, but would sometimes still be alive. I know, because I heard them whimpering. We learnt on the grapevine that Zyklon B took 20 minutes to kill its victims. However, because of the huge number of people coming in all the time, the camp authorities decided to speed things up by cutting the gassing time down to ten minutes.

This may have been the reason why some of the children were still alive when they came to be thrown into the furnace. Perhaps they hadn't been properly gassed. Perhaps, in the shock realisation of what was happening, their parents had clutched them to their bodies, burying the child's face against their naked skin. Perhaps, as the adults took the full force of the gas, they fell on top of the children, burying them against the ground and protecting them from the gas. Either way, they would still be breathing, still be alive, still be twitching, when they were brought to the incinerators for burning. They would whimper or moan quietly as the weight of the bodies on top of them was reduced, and they would still be living, even crying slightly, as they were hurled headlong into the furnaces.

The bodies were thrown in through an opening just above the stoking-hole. This would, I suppose, have been about 1.3 metres (four feet) off the ground. Because it would have taken too long to load the bodies into the furnace one at a time, a steel ramp, or chute, was angled into the entrance, and the bodies piled up on it. One person had a long pole with a steel plate on the end, which he used to push the bodies through the opening and into the furnace as they built up, in a sort of log-jam, at the entrance.

I have mentioned how children who had survived gassing were thrown live into the furnaces, but they weren't the only ones to suffer this fate. To understand these circumstances properly, you have to picture the death camp at Auschwitz–Birkenau as a sort of obscene factory, where the only product was death, and the ashes of death. For 24 hours of every day, weekends included, Auschwitz worked non-stop. There was a continuous frenzy of activity, with wagons of bodies being pushed at regular intervals from the gas chamber to the furnace, of empty wagons being pushed back, of wagons loaded with wood coming in from the forests to the wood pile and empty wagons being pushed back, of people loading wood onto smaller wagons and pushing them to the furnaces, and empty wagons being pushed back. Then there were the stokers, people like me, who worked in gangs of three, standing up all the time, taking one huge log at a time from the small stacks on each side of the furnace door and tossing them into the flames.

The entire camp operated with total efficiency, giving a fascinating insight into the German work ethic. During the '50s and '60s, when newly rebuilt, economically re-equipped Germany was the powerhouse of Europe — and, indeed, of the world — newspapers around the globe were full of stories about German efficiency and determination to succeed. Yes, the Germans are hard-working and yes, they do put meticulous planning into their work systems and factories. But, having seen the gruesome reality of Auschwitz, it is not drawing too long a bow to say that the death camp at Auschwitz, and others like it, provided a sort of a grim model of how an efficient factory should be run.

The factory analogy can be taken at least one step further, with the supervisory role played by the Capos. In a normal factory, the pressure to work hard, to be more productive, comes through incentive payments and productivity bonuses. At Auschwitz, the incentive to work harder was the stark realisation that if you didn't, you would be killed. The Capos watched over us to see that we didn't slacken, and SS guards, some with pistols in holsters, others with rifles, would watch over them. Then, 20 metres (60 feet) or so away would be more SS guards with submachine guns slung over their shoulders, ready to act if there was any sign of insurrection. It was a system of armed guards watching armed guards watching Capos watching desperate, human skeletons of prisoners.

The work was ghastly, exhausting and endless. We were poorly fed, receiving little more than a cup of watery swede soup twice a day. Disease was rife, with typhus, typhoid, tuberculosis, dysentery and a dozen other illnesses rampant. We were often dead on our feet, but if we had slowed down for a second, or allowed ourselves to be goaded into making a comment, saying something to the guards, rebelling at the Capos or telling them where to get off, death would have followed seconds later.

I saw it many times. We would be working at the furnace, keeping up as best we could, and some of the Poles, skinny, malnourished, racked with disease, would be little more than zombies. They would try to keep up, but they did not have the health and strength for the work. The Capos and the guards, always on the look-out for this sort of thing, would pounce immediately, ordering the slow-coach to be thrown into the furnace on the spot. It happened, and I saw it.

In the first couple of days alone, some 30 or 40 men assigned to my gang were unable to keep up and were tossed, headlong and breathing, into the furnace. I couldn't believe what I was seeing. Never in my wildest dreams had I imagined that people could behave that way, treating other human beings as though they were nothing more than a pinch of dust. I stood there with my mouth gaping open, almost in a trance, not knowing what to do or think, when one of the Poles I was working with nudged me with his shoulder. This broke the spell. I looked at the Pole and was about to say something like, 'What is it, mate?' or 'I can't believe all this,' when he shook his head and motioned me to get back to work, fast. He jerked his head towards the guards and the Capos, closed his eyes and gave a shiver, all of this with a look of naked terror on his face. The message came home loud and clear: do nothing, say nothing, keep your head down, and work.

We did find time to talk, however, at odd moments here and there during the day, when the guards and the Capos had their backs turned or their attention diverted. That's when the men I was working with would ask who I was, where Australia was, what it was like. I'd let my mind wander back to the sun and the wheat fields, to the beaches of Melbourne, to the wineries around Mildura, to my motorbikes, to Mum and Dad and my mates.

'You rich man,' they would say.

'No,' I'd reply, 'just ordinary, just a battler.'

'But you have good life. In Poland, in Germany, things very bad.'

'Australia is a good country,' I'd say. 'We grow our own food and there's plenty of sunshine and room for everyone.'

The term 'lucky country' hadn't been coined in those days or I'd have said, 'Australia? It's a lucky country.'

At first I tried to get to know the men I was working with, but the death rate was so high that it was a complete waste of time. After those first couple of days, when so many men were hurled into the roaring flames, they just became numbers to me: one and two, *eins* and *zwei* in German. To them I was 'Oss'. Not given a triangle to show my status as a prisoner, I wrote the word on my striped prison shirt with a finger dipped in ash. I'd told them, 'Call me Aussie,' but 'Oss' or 'Ossie' was the closest they could get to pronouncing it.

There was another reason why I stopped trying to remember the names of the men I worked with. After about three months of working on the furnaces, I became quite attached to one of the men, a skinny little Polish chap who seemed to have held on to a bit more of his character, a bit more of his dignity, than the others. We didn't talk much — couldn't talk — with the guards all around us waiting to strike, but somehow we formed a bond. There was something in his mannerisms that I took to, the way he rolled his eyes and shook his head, and shrugged his shoulders at what was going on. This was his way of living with death and horror every day, and I suppose it struck some sort of a chord in me. There was also something in me that he took to — possibly that I was such a foreigner. Anyway, we became mates, or as much as two people could become mates in that place.

I forget his name now, but I remember what he looked like: slightly built, slightly stooped, and with a thin face and expressive eyes. I also remember he wasn't well. At first he kept up well enough with the workload, but he soon weakened and after a week or so, perhaps longer, he was falling behind. At first the other man in the gang and I covered for him, working that bit harder, standing in front of him when he just stood there, unable to move, shielding him from the guards' prying gaze and their willingness to commit on-the-spot murder. But, eventually, the fatal combination of remorselessly hard, physical work and an unending diet of poor food took their toll, and he simply became too weak to carry on.

No matter what we did, there was no way we could cover for him any more. Then, one morning, the guards saw him standing there, not working, pathetically ill, dead on his feet, and screamed at him. They unslung their rifles and bashed him to the ground. Then they called the Capos over, just two of them, and gave the order. The Capos lifted him up and carried the little fellow the two, three, four paces to the furnace door. Just as they lifted him up to throw him in, he looked at me and his lips formed the word 'Ossie'.

I looked at him and shook my head, ever so slightly so the guards wouldn't see, to show that I could do nothing. The look on his face changed then, to what I can only describe as an expression of resigned understanding, and with that the Capos threw him in. He screamed, of course, for a second or two, as the flames engulfed him. A minute later he was barely recognisable as a human being.

I still have nightmares about that little man. In the months and years that I have been putting these memoirs together, his image has come back to me, night after night. The look on his face, the expression in those sad eyes, when he realised he had come to the end of the road, is something that will haunt me forever. Even now, as I write these words, I can see his face and I can't help crying.

I mentioned in the previous chapter how the guards and Capos liked to have a bit of 'fun' by picking on the weakest prisoners, chopping off their penis and then throwing them screaming into the furnace, followed by anyone who dared to protest — after they had been shot in the legs, that is. Well that, I am forced to say, is not the only 'sport' those bastards engaged in. There was another 'game' that was even more horrific for those involved, although it ended the same way. A regular occurrence in the camp would be the arrival of prisoners who, although they looked to be big and strong, would be a bit slow, a bit soft in the head, a bit simple.

They would be the sort of person who wouldn't realise that the guards were deadly earnest when they screamed at you to work. These people — soft, lazy, stupid, whatever — just wouldn't wake up to the fact that at Auschwitz it was work or die. So they would stand around, trying to hide behind other people so the guards wouldn't see them. Of course, the guards knew, or knew soon enough, when the Capos told them, and kept a special form of death in store.

The Capos would grab their victim and carry him screaming to the furnace door. Then, holding on to his arms and legs, they would put his head into the furnace, just for a few seconds, but long enough for his hair and scalp to catch fire and come up in the most appalling blisters. The Capos would then pull the person out of the furnace and leave him, head burning, to sit there and scream or run around in panic-stricken terror. If the person was lucky, he'd die after a few minutes, or collapse into unconsciousness and be thrown into the furnace. If the agony went on for any longer, the guards and the Capos, sadistic pigs each and every one of them, would look at him, point, and roar with laughter.

Sometimes they would fire a few bullets fired into the poor devil, say into his legs, just to add to the amusement. Then, when they had tired of their fun, the guards would give the word and the person, whether alive, dead or a gibbering wreck, would be tossed into the fires. And if you think that sort of thing only happened on an isolated basis, you are wrong. All the events I have written about here and in the preceding chapter happened constantly, several times a day, each day and every day. I know, because, as I have said before, I was there and I saw it.

When I say that we worked at the furnaces for 12 hours without a break, I mean that almost literally. We didn't stop — weren't allowed to stop — even for a call of nature, no matter how urgent that might be. If we had to piddle, we did it up against the side of the furnace when the guards weren't looking. For anything more urgent, we squatted down and did it in our food plate, mug, tin can or whatever we had, and threw it into the furnace. We then cleaned the plate as best we could, with a splash of water if we had any to spare (which wasn't often) or, more usually, by piddling on it. We used this same receptacle for lunch and dinner.

I was slightly luckier than most, because a friendly Russian who worked on the wagons taking bodies to the crematoria scrounged a water bottle for me. He also filled it for me every second day or so, and this helped me survive the dehydrating heat from the furnaces.

Anyway, we'd arrive at the furnace at six o'clock sharp, having eaten whatever scraps we had been given for breakfast. That would be it until noon. I used to keep my water bottle tied around my waist with a piece of string. I imagine it would have contained about a litre (a couple of pints) of water, and was the only liquid that I had for the day. For some reason that was never explained, there always seemed to be a water shortage at Auschwitz. There was certainly not enough to shower with, even though there was a shower block. I kept my water bottle on me at all times. If I had taken it off and left it somewhere, even for a few minutes, it would have been stolen, and I'd have had Buckley's chance of getting another one. You learnt these things as you went along.

The only break in the whole of the 12-hour shift was at noon, when we would break for half an hour or however long it took to walk to the kitchens on the south side of the camp. There, a huge pot of watery swede or turnip soup awaited us (I was soon to find out that this horrid, tasteless gruel was pretty much the staple diet at Auschwitz–Birkenau). That was the only break we had in the entire day, that short walk to the kitchen and back. When I hear people today, with their breaks for morning coffee, afternoon tea, lunch, and regular smokos on the pavement outside the office or in the smoking room at the factory, say how hard they work, I sometimes find it hard not to smile.

We knocked off work at six o'clock sharp each day, just as punctually as we had started. We would then trudge back to our barracks via the kitchen, where we received yet another ladle of watery soup in the same tin can, mug or bowl we had been defecating into. If we were lucky, there would be a crust of bread as well. We would take this back to the hut and eat it as slowly as possible, making sure we derived maximum benefit from these starvation rations. Then, after perhaps talking for a few minutes to the people around us, we would fall into an exhausted sleep, on the ground, right up against the next person. About 100 of us slept together, without a blanket between us, regardless of weather or season, in a hut measuring roughly five metres (16 feet) by three metres (nine feet).

I lived like this, month after month, surrounded by disease-ridden men who were often so weak that they died in their sleep. We would carry their bodies out in the morning. The general state of health was appalling. On those nights when I couldn't sleep for one reason or another, I'd lie there listening to the men around me coughing their guts up or vomiting, the weak ones defecating where they lay. Others would wake up in the middle of the night and use the latrine can at the end of the room. I would lie there, gasping for breath, sick to the stomach with all the death and brutality that was taking place around me. That's when I'd start to think of Australia and the good times I'd had before I joined up. Jeez, it made me want to cry, but I think it kept me sane.

The question I have asked myself more than any other since I started these memoirs is: how did I remain sane? I don't have an easy answer to that. Some prisoners became so sickened by what was happening around them that they deliberately provoked the guards into shooting them. Others threw themselves at the electrified fence around the perimeter of the camp and died instantly. I think I got through each day by switching off mentally, by doing the work I was forced to do, and by shutting out the grisly nature of what was happening around me, or at least not letting it register.

I noticed dimly, at the back of my mind, what the weather was like from day to day, but whether it was windy, raining, or gloriously sunny was not something that gave me any pleasure. How can you take pleasure from the simple things of life when you are a imprisoned thousands of miles from home, unable to talk to family, friends and loved ones, and have to stare death in the face every day? How can you take pleasure in anything, when you have armed guards standing over you, forcing you to carry out horrendous acts of barbarity day after day?

The last thing I would have done — the last thing anyone ever thought of doing — was to nudge a workmate, give him a big smile and say, 'Nice day!' Nice day? In Auschwitz? To appreciate a nice day, to take delight in the warmth of the sun, the gentleness of a breeze and the soft kiss of rain, you have to be free, free to stand straight, free to hold your head high, not to be cowed and bowed, and stood over by bullies and tyrants. It was the same with colours — after a while I just didn't notice colours any more. To talk of colours and take pleasure in them requires a peaceful, reflective and receptive state of mind. In Auschwitz our minds were concentrated on just one thing: staying alive.

Another reason why I survived, I think, was that I had learnt to handle pain. The fact that I had had a hernia operation without anaesthetic at Stalag 13C had taught me how to overcome pain. So had the brutal beating I received at the hands of the police and the Gestapo when they interrogated me. Of course, if I hadn't been able to handle pain so well — if I'd talked my head off and sung like a canary while being interrogated — I wouldn't have been in Auschwitz at all.

During the hernia operation, I focused my mind on the good, happy, carefree days of my youth, and the larrikin times I'd had with my mates. These memories kept me going in Auschwitz, too. But more than that, surviving in Auschwitz was simply a case of hardening your mind and your heart to what was going on. I think this is the voice of survival speaking here, because I was determined to do everything within my power to survive. I wasn't going to let the bastards get me down! The fact that I lived 44 years after my release from Auschwitz without telling a soul is some proof of this. But don't get me wrong, I am not a callous person and I can't stand bullying or cruelty of any sort. Physical abuse and violence are abhorrent to me.

Of course there were times when I wanted to cry out, to stop the madness that was occurring around me. I wanted to scream every second of every day. But what good would that have done me? It wouldn't have stopped the carnage at Auschwitz, and I would have been butchered on the spot — thrown live into the furnaces like so many others every day. And what good would that have done? It's a cliche, but I feel somehow that during my seven months at Auschwitz — two months in the underground cell and five months stoking the furnaces — my philosophy must have been that while there was life there was hope. That's how I was able to hang on. Then again, maybe I simply had a charmed life, or was born under a lucky star.

I was in two minds for some time about whether to include the following details in my Auschwitz–Birkenau memoirs, but finally decided to do so because I know what I saw and I also know what I was told.

On several occasions, particularly towards the start of my time at Auschwitz, wagon-loads of bodies would be brought over to the furnaces, and the word went around that they were from 'Schindler'. I had no idea what, or who, Schindler was. The matter-of-fact way it was stated made me think it was a town. You have to understand, I had no knowledge of Polish and only a rudimentary knowledge of German. To me, one word, one name, one place name, was just like another. So, when I heard these bodies came from Schindler, I assumed it was a town and thought no more of it.

Then, around 1990, at a POW reunion dinner, I got talking to an old friend of mine from the 2/7th Battalion, Charlie Garth, who had spent some time working in a Nazi factory just outside Krakow. I was able to discuss my war-time experiences by then, at least in a limited way, and Charlie mentioned the terrible smell that hung in the air around Krakow every day — a smell so bad that at times, even at the height of summer, they couldn't open the windows. 'It was a really rotten, sickening smell,' said Charlie. 'They said it came from Auschwitz, 25 kilometres (15 miles) away.'

It was around this time, too, that newspapers and magazines started carrying stories about *Schindler's List*, the film Steven Spielberg was making, based on Tom Keneally's book *Schindler's Ark*. Out of the blue, and with no prompting from me, Charlie said he had heard about Schindler because the factory where he was working in Poland was only about

100 metres (300 feet) from Schindler's factory. Charlie said that everyone he worked with knew about Schindler, and talked about the deals he was doing with the Nazis. It was common knowledge that only the best, the strongest Jewish workers were sent to work at Schindler's. That's when what I knew about Schindler started to fall into place. Confirming what I had heard in Auschwitz, Charlie said that when Schindler's workers weakened and could no longer do a day's work, the SS sent them off to Auschwitz and straight to the gas chamber.

I have not read Tom Keneally's book, but I have seen *Schindler's List* and I can't say that I was impressed. My perception of Oskar Schindler is at some variance with the character of the wealthy industrialist portrayed in the film. From what I heard, it seems that Schindler was a ruthless entrepreneur, a schemer who did deals with the Nazis to obtain slave labour for his factory near Krakow. My understanding is that Schindler worked his Jewish labour force tirelessly and, when they dropped or were unable to put in a full day's work, he consigned them to the care of the SS, who sent them to the camp at nearby Auschwitz and had replacements sent in as quickly as possible.

It is not my intention in writing this to denigrate or in any way dismiss the painstaking research that Tom Keneally put into *Schindler's Ark,* a book for which he won the Booker Prize for literature in 1982. He is and remains an eminent Australian and a world-class author. But my experience with the name Schindler was quite different from his, and my impression of the man based on what I heard at the time.

CHAPTER 8
Liberation

At the end of November 1944, I was suddenly taken off the furnaces. Two guards came along one day and told me to put down my shovel, then escorted me to an office in the administration block, where I was told to wait. I didn't know what to think. Questions without answers raced through my mind. What had I done? What was the matter? Was I going to be executed? If so, what for? Why didn't they just throw me into the furnace? And the expressions on my Polish mates' faces when the guards took me away! They weren't expecting me back, that's for sure.

I was left standing for two hours, and when the guards came out they told me bluntly that I was being sent to an Australian POW camp. I thought, 'Oh yeah? That's a likely story.' I must have looked stupid, standing there, with no expression on my face. The guards started shouting at me: 'Do you understand, Englishman? You are leaving here. You are going to a prisoner-of-war camp. You will be with your own people. You are leaving Auschwitz!'

A feeling of unreality swept through me, followed by an incredible sense of relief. For a few minutes, while the full impact of what they had told me sank in, all the fears and worries, all the pain and suffering, the hardships and the heartbreaks of the past seven months ebbed from me. Broken down, wretched, unbelievably skinny and in rotten health though I was, I felt a new man. No reasons, no explanations were given as to why I was being moved. All I know is that I got out of that office fast, in case they changed their minds! I really had thought, in my darkest moments of lice-ridden despair, that I would never get out of that hellish place alive. The sad thing was that I wasn't able to get word to the two Poles I was working with. Had I tried, they would have been killed for sure.

With my head still reeling, I was loaded into the back of a truck and driven west, into Germany and towards the advancing Allied armies. After three days on the road, three days of dodging Allied aircraft that flew overhead, bombing roads and railways, we arrived at a POW camp near Hanover. Nothing was said to me, not a word, and I was thrown into a cell for two days. Then, joy of joys, I was taken out and given a shower — my first in eight months! Was I in heaven? I certainly thought so as warm water sprayed over my head. And my body — it was actually clean!

They gave me an English uniform to put on, and a little food. The uniform was miles too big for me: I'd shrunk to barely 50 kilograms (120 pounds), and must have looked a sight. But I was wearing clean clothes, proper boots, and socks for the first time in ages. It felt wonderful. While I was trying to keep some food down — my stomach had shrunk so much that digestion was difficult — I started reflecting on the Auschwitz experience and how, in some warped, perverted way, what I had seen as my incredible bad luck in being sent to Auschwitz, after being interrogated by the sadistic bastard who smashed my fingers back at Nuremberg, may actually have been my salvation.

Because my hands were like two lumps of raw meat by the time he had finished with me, I had been unable to work. Because of that, I had been put into a cell and, as a result, had probably escaped the gas chamber. Was it that simple, that easy? I don't know. Even to this day, I don't know. Had the decision been taken right from the start that I was to be regarded as a prisoner of war, that no matter how brutal the

treatment at Auschwitz, no matter how weak or sick I became, there was no way they were going to kill me outright?
All I knew, as I sat there in Hanover, in my ridiculously large
uniform, was that I was alive. I had clean clothes and was
being sent to join my countrymen. If that constitutes con-
tentment of the human soul, then I was content indeed. I was
a happy man.

I don't know which POW camp it was that they sent
me to near Hanover. My mind was still too full of the murder
and suffering I had seen all around me over the past seven
months to take in the details. I do know, however, that my
new mates regarded me as a weird one. Despite that first
shower, I couldn't seem to get the smell of death off me. Every
time I put my hands to my face, I could smell death on my
fingers. I would stand at the tap for ages, washing my hands
over and over. Eventually one of the men came over and said,
'What's up, mate? What's the matter?' I replied, 'Oh, nothing.
I'm not real well. I've been sick for a while, in hospital.' And
they left it at that.

There were a few blokes there that I had been with in
Torun, in Poland, but I had changed so much that no-one
recognised me. Out of curiosity, I made contact with the camp's
escape committee. I recognised a few chaps there, but no-one
knew who I was until I started speaking. Then, one of them
recognised my voice. 'Is that Don Watt?' he said. 'Is that really
you, Don?' Next, they all wanted to know what had happened,
and where I had been since I made my run from Torun. They'd
known that they would have heard from me if I'd made it to
England, but it had been nine months since I had escaped,
and they wanted the details. They also explained to me that
they had been moved into Germany a few months earlier,
when it became clear that the Germans were losing the war
and that Poland was going to be overrun by the advancing
Russian army.

I gave them the full details of my escape, and how I had
been on the run for three weeks before being captured near
the Swiss border. However, instead of saying anything about
Auschwitz, I said I had become seriously ill and had spent

several months in hospital. They only needed to take one look at me to see that I had lost a great deal of weight, and they said things like, 'Oh, bad luck mate. We were hoping you would make it back home,' and left it at that. From that day on, for 44 years, I didn't mention a word about Auschwitz to anybody.

No matter how much I washed my hands, I still stank of death. No-one else commented on it, so I knew it had to be in my mind. To me, I reeked of death. It was in my guts, in every pore. My skin was still permeated with the stench of burning human flesh. I had been breathing that smell without a break for the whole five months I was on the furnaces. It was so bad, that nothing smelled clean or natural. Even the water smelled off.

I got a lot of stares from my new mates at that time. I didn't talk much, and although I tried to smile at their jokes and various antics, it just wasn't in me. The blokes had no idea what I'd been through, and I couldn't tell them about it. I spent hours upon hours by myself, staring into space or washing my hands, and I could see that my mates thought I was cracking up. Maybe I was, but I couldn't tell them why. How do you tell someone that you have just spent seven months of your life stoking a furnace so that some of the most barbarous people the world has seen could burn the dead bodies of thousands upon thousands of innocent people whom they had murdered in the most sickening of circumstances?

Even if I'd been able to tell them, how could they have believed me? How could anyone who had not experienced such atrocities understand what it was like to be there? They'd have thought I'd cracked for sure, even if I only hinted at what I'd been through.

Five months later, in April 1945, and with Field Marshall Montgomery's 7th Armoured Division making good progress through the routed German lines, the prison guards at the Hanover camp received orders to march all POWs further east. I'd had more than enough of the Germans by then, and was heartily sick and tired of taking their orders and having them shouting at me. When the word was given to move out, I hid in a hole I'd made under the hut, creeping out after two days and heading west, desperately trying to avoid the re-treating German troops.

After two days on the run, I hid out in a large tin shed and was surprised to find it full of rice, tons and tons of it, piled up in bags. There was so much food, I couldn't believe it. It had survived, I was told later by another POW, because everyone thought the hut was an ammunition dump. No-one had bothered to look inside, and the soldiers who had stored the rice there had neglected to tell anyone — a typical army stuff-up.

After two more days on the road, constantly dodging demoralised Germans, I ran into a British tank brigade and joined one of the crews. They were a bit suspicious of me at first, as they had been told to be on the look-out for Germans masquerading in Allied uniforms. They soon realised, however, that I was the genuine article. For my part, it was great to be with some active servicemen again. They wanted to know why I was so thin, so I simply said there hadn't been much food in the POW camps. That seemed to satisfy them, and they didn't pursue the matter. They were very generous blokes, those English soldiers, and readily shared their rations with me. Among other things, they gave me half a loaf of white bread — the first I'd seen since being taken prisoner by the Germans on Crete. The bread smelled really good, but all I could do was nibble the odd piece. I still had the smell of death about me, and my stomach had shrunk so much that the smallest amount of food filled me up in no time. Even half a glass of water would have done it.

The tank crews were on the look-out for German soldiers who might be hiding out with weapons and ammunition to stage some form of rear-guard action, and it was clear from the start that they weren't taking any chances. On one occasion, we came to a village where a few Germans had taken over a farmhouse. As soon as our tank came into view, they opened

fire on us with machine-guns and bazookas. The tank commander didn't mess about.

The instant the bullets and shells started whizzing
around, he turned the turret of the tank towards the farmhouse
and gave the word for a single shell to be fired. That was all it
took. The shell smashed clean through the front door and
out the back wall. Seconds later, a couple of cats came bolting
out, then a dog, and a couple of chooks. It was like something
from an old Dad 'n Dave movie. Finally, a white flag was waved
though the front door and the fighting was over.

It was my guess that there might be more POWs back
at the camp near Hanover, so the major in charge detached a
tank to go and investigate. We found about 200 men still
hiding out in the camp, bags of bones every one of them, but
none as skinny as I was. The blokes in the tank were terribly
moved. They had never seen anything like it, not on such a
large scale. They reached into their ration bags and handed
out a few fresh loaves and some bars of chocolate.

'Look at the poor buggers,' they said. 'Human skeletons.
Those bloody Germans! Bastards! Fancy treating another
human being that way. Soldiers, too. If I get my hands on
them, I'll show them a thing or two!' I listened with my mouth
shut and said nothing. 'Mate,' I thought, 'You haven't seen
anything. I could tell you things that would make the blood
drain from your face.' But I kept quiet. What was the point of
talking about it? Besides, I wanted to forget.

We formed patrols to look for German stragglers, and
combed the surrounding countryside and a couple of nearby
villages. The Germans had all retreated, but we did find a few
Russians, part of an advance party of Russian troops who had
come on ahead from the east. Two of them were rough-
handling a couple of teenage girls aged 16 or so — it was easy
to see what they were after — when suddenly there was a
mighty scream.

I ran towards the sound and found another Russian
trying to rape an old woman — the girls' grandmother, as it
turned out. I shouted at him to pack it in and to let the woman
go, but he turned and pointed a gun at me. I didn't like the

look of that, and I couldn't come at an old woman being raped — or any woman being raped for that matter, I'm just not that sort of person — so I pulled out my service revolver in a flash and shot him on the spot. The women thanked me and ran off. About an hour or so later we ran into a Russian patrol, and I explained to them what had happened and how I had just shot one of their fellow countrymen. They were obviously a decent bunch of blokes, because they took it surprisingly well, which was a load off my mind. Any other Russians might have shot me.

Getting back to England was a bit of a lark. One of the English soldiers I had talked to on the tank had said that you could make a fair bit of money —a few thousand pounds — by driving a German car, preferably a Mercedes, back to Paris and selling it to the boys on leave. So, with another Aussie, I found a Merc, pumped up the tyres, filled the tank and headed west again. All went well until we came to a British road block and the insurmountable barrier of British bloody-mindedness.

'You can't come through here. Not with that car,' said the soldier in charge. 'Why not?' I asked. 'Orders,' he said. 'We've got orders not to let anyone through in a motor vehicle, unless they've got written permission from their commanding officer.'

My mate and I started to protest. 'Oh, come on,' he said. 'Listen, we're a couple of Australian POWs. We've spent four years in a POW camp and we've just been liberated. All we're trying to do is get to Paris and have a good time, have a few beers, meet a few girls, have a few laughs. You know how it is. Come on, mate, let us through!'

It was a waste of time talking to him. There was no way the Brits were going to allow us through. They weren't even interested in talking to us, so we drove along a few side roads hoping to find a way through, but without luck. Every road was blocked and every soldier minding the road blocks seemed to take evil delight in being difficult. Feeling totally frustrated, we doubled back to the first road block, picking up a machine-gun on the way, and telling ourselves that if the Brits wouldn't let us through, we'd bluff them into thinking we would shoot our way past. That was the plan, anyway.

We arrived back at the first road block and tried talking to the soldiers in a friendly way, but again they wouldn't listen. We again explained that we had been prisoners of war for four years and we were trying to get to Paris, but this meant nothing to them. We got back into the car and my mate pulled out the machine-gun.

'All right,' he said. 'We've tried being nice about it. Now if you don't shift that bloody road block, we'll bloody well shoot our way through and you're going to get it first!' With that, English soldiers emerged out of nowhere, pointing submachine guns at us, their fingers on the trigger. We were surrounded. We didn't have a chance and we knew it, but my mate was determined they weren't going to get their hands on our lovely car.

With the Brits covering us, he put his machine-gun down and made a big show of saying we had only been joking. Then, with the Poms still pointing their guns at him, he flipped open the bonnet and tossed in a grenade. You should have seen their faces when the engine blew up! We told them that they could get rid of the wreck and walked through the road block as cool as ice. Without the car, they couldn't have cared less about us. We were browned off, though. All that money we could have made by selling the car in Paris had literally gone up in smoke, just because of handful of stubborn Poms. Feeling very dejected, we walked along the road for a couple of miles, until an army truck came along and gave us a lift to an airfield, where we boarded a plane to Paris.

Paris was in chaos. Parisians were still full of joy that the Germans had been kicked out of their beloved city three months earlier, but the grim reality of how to survive in the new liberated order was also beginning to sink in, and the city was in turmoil. The men who had run the Resistance movement were coming forward all the time to denounce those who had collaborated with the Nazis under the Vichy regime. This was causing acute embarrassment to the French and the Americans, as many collaborators were very highly placed.

The communists were also riding high. They had formed the backbone of the Resistance and were now positioning themselves for the spoils and rewards of peace. Against this tumultuous background, ordinary people were trying to live, trying to put their lives back together, trying to find loved ones who had been missing for years. And everyone, Resistance workers, communists, ordinary people, were desperately rushing around trying to find work and to buy cheap food instead of paying horrendously inflated black-market prices. Others were trying to put their wrecked homes together in a city starved of building materials. No-one had much money and everyone seemed to be living on hope.

Not having much to do, I wandered down to a British servicemen's canteen, or NAAFI, as they called them, which is short for Navy, Army and Air Force Institutes. I was having a cup of tea and a sandwich (a cuppa and a wad, the Brit soldiers called it), when the canteen lady came over for a chat. Her name was Robin (I can't remember her family name) and, naturally enough, she wanted to know why I was so thin. I gave her the POW story about how scarce food had been, and she got me another cuppa. I told Robin she was the first English-speaking woman I had talked to for four years. I must have looked a bit silly, being a skinny bloke inside a huge uniform. She laughed with me in a kind, friendly, sympathetic way and we chatted on. Eventually she asked if I'd like to see Paris.

'Listen, Don,' she said. 'Unless you have plans, or orders, or you want to be on your way as quickly as possible, why don't you stay in Paris for a while? I know my way around quite well and I'd love to show you the city and sights, and introduce you to some of the life. That's if you're interested. Of course, if you'd rather be with your mates . . . '.

'Interested?' I said. 'Robin, I can't think of anything I'd rather do. I'm not under any orders except to make my way back to England eventually and present myself to the Australian authorities. So far as mates are concerned, I don't know anyone in Paris at all. So if you're happy to show me around, I'd love it. And thanks very much for asking.'

I stayed a week. Robin knew plenty of places, and we went around a great deal, seeing different people as well as taking in the sights of the Eiffel Tower, the Arc de Triomphe and Napoleon's Tomb. We also went for long walks along the Seine, through the Luxembourg Gardens and the Tuileries. I was struck by the size and the beauty of Paris. Melbourne was the biggest city I had seen up till then, and the beauty of Paris was mind-blowing. I also tried using my schoolboy French, but no-one could understand a word I said, apart from *deux bières* when I wanted a couple of beers, and that was only because I held up two fingers. And to think I'd been getting 90 per cent for French at school! Something had to be wrong.

Robin introduced me to a French family who must have been quite rich before the war. They were still pretty wealthy and went to a great deal of trouble to turn on a traditional French dinner for me, complete with snails and frogs' legs and, naturally, plenty of garlic. It looked excellent, but I was still having trouble keeping anything but the lightest food down. I had never eaten French food before, but there was no way I could do justice to what was clearly a magnificent feast. I had to apologise. I think they were a little disappointed but they were all very understanding.

I have to say that Robin was one of the most delightful women I have ever met. I'd like to think we could have had a relationship, even a permanent one, but at that time, and in my condition, I was simply not interested. On one occasion, when we were having a drink at a pavement cafe near the Arc de Triomphe, Robin remarked how impressed she was that I didn't take advantage of a lady.

'Robin,' I said, 'there's nothing I'd rather do than get to know you more intimately, because you are one of the sweetest women I have ever met. I'm not queer, if that's what you are wondering, but so far as a bit of nooky's concerned, well, I'm just not interested. I mean I'm interested, but I'm not up to that sort of thing. Not yet anyway. I'm just not ready for it.'

She must have thought I was downright peculiar. I mean, whoever heard of a Aussie soldier — let alone one who hadn't so much as seen a woman for years — passing up an opportunity like this? But she smiled and said she understood.

After a week, I met an Australian pilot who offered me a ride to England. This was what I had been waiting for, and I thanked Robin for her generosity and hospitality. We gave each other a big hug. 'You're a weird one, Don Watt,' she said. 'A nice man, but weird. I won't forget you.' With that, we kissed and I was on my way.

We first flew to Brussels, where the pilot had special orders to deliver, and took the opportunity to look around the city. We went into the centre of town, where big celebrations were taking place for Belgian servicemen who had returned home, and joined in the fun at a couple of cafes or bistros. It was good to see people happy again, and it was good to be happy with them. We took off for England the next day.

The English had suffered a lot during the war, more than many Australians appreciated at the time, what with food shortages and the constant bombing of London and other major cities during the Blitz, but their spirit was wonderful. The pilot radioed ahead to say he had an Aussie POW on board, and the people at the airfield put the red carpet out for me. From the moment I landed, they could not have been nicer and I was made to feel really at home. I was taken to a room for delousing and then to an aircraft hangar, where a lovely meal had been prepared for me, including chocolate and drinks. I thanked them warmly because things were still tight in England, and they had gone to a lot of trouble, but again I had to explain that I wasn't ready for really solid food. That night I was given a bed with clean, fresh sheets. A luxury.

In England I spent most of my time at Eastbourne, a seaside town on the south coast, where the Australian

Headquarters (Staging Base) was established. They wanted me to go through a debriefing session, but mentally I wasn't ready for it. I told them I'd been so badly beaten up at the interrogation centre in Nuremberg that I had to be taken to hospital, where various complications had set in, and I'd become seriously ill. It was clear from my attitude that I didn't want to discuss it and happily they left it at that. I certainly made no mention of Belsen and Auschwitz, because that was one part of the war I desperately wanted to forget.

Up to that point I had been unable to put on weight. This was starting to worry the doctors, and I was having one medical check-up after another. Eventually one doctor had a brainwave. 'The best thing you can do, chum,' he said, 'is have a few bottles of Guinness every day. That'll improve your appetite and you'll be putting on weight in no time.' Well, that sounded like a very good idea (I like doctors who prescribe drinking as a cure), and I started off by drinking four small bottles a day. Sure enough, my appetite soon came back and I was able to eat a little more each day. Before long, I was having a meal every four hours. Talk about putting on weight! Crikey — I put on nearly 19 kilograms (40 pounds). As it happens, this wasn't such a good thing, and the strangest things started happening to me. My legs puffed up and my feet swelled so much that I couldn't put my boots on. I didn't know what was happening to me, so I made arrangements to see the doctor.

'You may find this surprising, Corporal Watt, but you have beriberi,' the doctor told me.

'Oh, come on, Doc,' I said. 'That's a tropical disease, isn't it? You hear about people in India suffering from beriberi. I've never been to India in my life. Ceylon, on the way over from Australia. But that was only for a few days. Not long enough to get beriberi, surely.'

The doctor smiled.

'That's a popular misconception,' he said. 'Beriberi is caused by a lack of thiamine — vitamin B1. You can get it if you don't have enough protein in your diet. Enough fish, meat, eggs and cheese. That sort of thing. You said you spent a lot of time in the POW camps. What did they feed you there?'

'Oh, watery soup most of the time, with turnips and swedes, that sort of thing. A bit of cheese occasionally, not often.'

'But didn't you get any Red Cross parcels? That's the whole idea of the parcels, to make sure you get some decent food that will help prevent disease.'

I just shrugged. What was I going to say? Tell him I'd been in Auschwitz, and the closest thing to fresh meat I'd seen in seven months was a fly on the wall? I shrugged again and said nothing.

One day I visited a large hotel, where they had separate rooms for darts, cards and so on, and one that contained a piano so people could have a sing-along. I was singing away and having a bottle of Guinness when I noticed an aroma that I hadn't smelled in years — women's perfume. I looked around, saw the lady who was wearing it, and told her what a lovely smell it was. I gave her my POW story and asked if she had the scent bottle with her because, if she did, I'd like a really good sniff. She looked at me as though I'd escaped from a nut-house and produced the scent bottle from her handbag. I took the top off and gave it a good sniff. It was so good that I went back to the hotel the next day to see if the woman was still there. She was, so I asked for another sniff. I'm sure Robin wore perfume back in Paris, but I didn't notice it. That perfume in Eastbourne was the first smell to break through the barrier of the stench of human flesh that was still in my mind and, I thought, on my body.

I was in England for two months and took in some West End shows, including *Arsenic and Old Lace*, at the Strand Theatre, and some of the shows at the Windmill Theatre, which had kept going right through the war. Their motto was, 'We never close,' and they didn't, no matter what Goering and the Luftwaffe threw at London. I went to the Windmill several times and got to know one of the staff, who took me back stage and introduced me to the floor manager. I was invited to stop after the show and join the entertainers when they had a few drinks and let their hair down. I had a lovely time. They told jokes and did some impersonations, and we all finished up having a sing-song. It was better than the real show.

While I was at Eastbourne, someone (probably a junior officer with little to do) had the not-very-bright idea of getting the POWs to do some marching drills. Well, we nearly mutinied. There were a few hundred of us ex-POWs there, and we quickly made it clear that we weren't having any of that. We told them there would be a riot if they tried it. The subject was never raised again. We were, however, expected to perform light duties, including going on goodwill missions, which meant showing the flag for Australia. One such mission was to Buckingham Palace, where I was fortunate to meet King George VI and Queen Elizabeth (the Queen Mother, as she is now), and the two princesses, Elizabeth and Margaret. They were only young girls then, of course.

Other duties involved looking after new POWs when they arrived from Europe, and getting them billeted in two streets of houses specifically allocated for POWs. By the time they had settled in, the mail had started flowing again and they were able to catch up with the news from home. Sometimes the news wasn't so good, such as when some soldiers heard that their girlfriends had chucked them over or had got married. One Aussie, a popular man as I recall, took it very badly and committed suicide in the fernery at the back of the house.

Others were so pleased to be out of the POW camps, that they went on benders and fell in love with the first girl they saw. One man got so drunk he actually married a big, fat English girl. We all told him not to be so silly, but he got the commanding officer to sign the papers and they were married in a registry office. The next morning, he realised what he had done, grabbed his trousers and bolted. He told us later that he had woken up, had a good look at her and thought, 'What the bloody hell have I done?' But when he told her to buzz off and that he wasn't having anything to do with her, she just waved the marriage certificate at him. I can't recall the man's name, but he was able to get the marriage annulled, although it cost him every penny of the money he had saved up in the years he had been a POW.

My time at Eastbourne let me see how being a POW affected different men in different ways. Although most of the men seemed to have taken it in their stride, others were profoundly upset by what they'd seen and heard. Sometimes it only took a couple of drinks for them to think they were back behind barbed wire. Take Cocky Walpole.

Cocky and I went to a dance in Eastbourne one Saturday. We were dancing, drinking a few beers and generally having a night of it when, all of a sudden, Cocky pulled out two Luger pistols and started shooting into the ceiling. Fortunately I knew Cocky well, so I pretended to be a bit drunk.

'Come on, Cocky,' I said. 'Give me a gun and I'll help you finish off the German bastards.' He looked at me in a daze and handed over one of the guns. I then took the other one from him and slowly walked him out of the dance hall. He spent two days in the military hospital getting over it. The nurses called it delayed shock, or something like that. By the time Cocky was okay, he didn't remember the incident at all.

I took leave on one occasion to visit George Timmis, the Cockney POW I'd met in Stalag 13C and who had been repatriated with a crook leg. He was back in his home town, Surbiton, south of London, and I took a kit bag of food with me. Was he surprised to see me! We went down to the local pub and yarned away for hours. I also got talking to the man who ran the pub and had a brainwave: how about closing off George's street for a street party? The publican said it shouldn't be too much trouble, and that he'd be happy to help me do it so long as we got the beer from him. We decided to hold the party the following Saturday.

With two Aussie mates, I travelled down to Surbiton with two big kit bags, each filled with tins of meat, butter, canned fruit and plenty of lollies for the kids. Someone had a portable wind-up gramophone and a whole stack of records, and that night the whole street joined in the celebrations, dancing and singing and having a good time. I talked to a lot of the people who lived in the street, and they said it was the first party they'd been to since the outbreak of war in 1939. My mate and I enjoyed ourselves too, if only to see the looks of delight on the children's faces. Some of them had never seen lollies.

I also went to Brighton for a couple of days. The idea was to go for a swim, because I'd met so many English soldiers who had raved on about Brighton. I thought I had to go there as it had to be something special. Well, so much for Brighton! The beach was all pebbles — not a grain of sand in sight! 'How on earth can they say they have a nice time at Brighton when there's no sand?' I thought. 'If they want to see a beach, they should come to Australia.' I walked along the beach, fully clothed, just to get the feel of the place. But I certainly didn't take my boots off.

To me, the best part of Brighton was the local dance hall, where you booked a table when you arrived. There was a bar and a bottle shop — off-licence, the English call them — and I was loaned a pair of dancing shoes by the band, as I was wearing army boots. Victor Sylvester's band was playing. It was the best dance band in England at the time, so I was told, and I danced with some of the musicians' wives. It was good to be on a dance floor again.

By now, end-of-war fever was starting to grip England. I managed to get leave for VE day and was looking forward to getting up to London, where I was sure the party would rage for hours. However, it seemed that I wouldn't be able to get anywhere near Trafalgar Square, where the main celebrations would be held. People had been piling into the centre of London for three days and it was already packed out. I suddenly had a brainstorm and decided to go to Scotland instead. Don Roy, who had worked with me before the war at the fruit packaging plant at Irymple and lived just across the road, had given me his parents' address in Dunkeld. I sent them a telegram and told them when I'd be arriving.

I took a train to Edinburgh, and then went the rest of

the way by bus. As luck would have it, the bus went through the village of Watt, so I thought I'd look up Dad's family. I told the bus driver, and he wanted to know which particular family I was interested in. I told him I was looking for the Watt family, but he said that every family there was called Watt. Unfortunately I didn't have the time to trace where Dad's branch of the family lived, so I decided to give it a miss.

Don Roy's family had been saving their petrol coupons so the family car had a full tank. We decided to celebrate in Glasgow, about two hours' drive away, found a pub and got stuck in, drinking beer with whisky chasers. Before long, bottles of Scotch were appearing from everywhere. We had a wonderful time, singing 'Knees Up Mother Brown' all night and lots of other songs, such the 'Hokey Pokey', or 'Hokey Kokey', as it's known in Britain. I think I was the only Aussie in the whole of Glasgow that night, certainly the only one in uniform, and everyone wanted to know me and buy me a drink. I've never seen so much Scotch, or drunk so much in one session. We had such a lot left, even after the long night of revelry, that we were able to fill the back seat of the car with bottles and take them back to Dunkeld. The celebrations there were just starting when we arrived. With our supplies, we were able to keep the town going for two days.

I stopped in London for a few days on the way back to Eastbourne and did the sights — Westminster Abbey, St Paul's Cathedral, Tower Bridge, the Houses of Parliament and Trafalgar Square — as well as a fair bit of exploring on the Tube and on the top deck of London's big, red, double-decker buses. I stayed at the Charing Cross Hotel — an easy place to find, even in a blackout — and went to Australia House in The Strand a couple of times to get a hot meal in the downstairs section. I also had a few good sessions in *The Codgers*, a pub in Fleet Street that's just around the corner from Reuters, the international news agency. Aussies had pretty well adopted the pub, and the colour patches of the Australian units were displayed around the walls and behind the bar. It was a regular meeting place for our boys.

Writing about *The Codgers* makes me think of the cafe

on the opposite side of the road — *Dirty Dicks*. The word was that you could always get a steak in this place, even in the middle of the Blitz, so with a couple of other blokes I decided to give it a go. I nipped out the back to use their toilets and on the way I saw the kitchen staff cutting up a great lump of horse meat. I should have known. I really should have known.

It wasn't long after this that I started to think of home. I had put on weight, my health was recovering — I was much stronger — and I felt it was time to be on my way. I suppose I was feeling homesick. I applied for the next draft to Australia and eventually left England from Liverpool, on board the SS *Stirling Castle*, bound for Sydney via the Panama Canal and Wellington.

I was looking forward to being back in Australia for the whole of the homeward voyage and, as we entered Sydney Heads, with the Harbour Bridge up ahead, my heart was in my mouth. I was home at last and, oh boy, how good it felt to be back on Australian soil. I didn't stay long in Sydney — it wasn't my town — and was soon making arrangements to get a train to Melbourne, then on to the big homecoming at Irymple. It was a great moment, especially to see my parents again after all this time and everything I had been through.

The trouble with the Army — or one of the troubles with the Army, I should say — is that everything concerning the troops is done alphabetically, and as my surname begins with a 'W', I was always one of the last. This wasn't so bad if it was extra duties that had to be done, but it also meant I was among the last to get my money on pay day and, on more than one occasion, by the time I had collected my money all the beer had gone! It also meant that I was among the last to be discharged.

Despite this, the weeks sped by, with me travelling back and forth between Irymple and Royal Park, and with endless visits to hospitals to have my nose fixed and get my knee seen to. It hadn't been right since it was hit by that lump of shrapnel on Crete. It was also good to bump into old mates, some of whom I hadn't seen since North Africa. But there was one meeting with a fellow soldier that I didn't enjoy at all.

It happened one day when Don Jones came rushing up to me at Royal Park, saying there was a chap waiting to see me in a nearby pub. Don was so keen to get going that we jumped into a taxi and headed off.

When we got there, a fellow sitting on a stool at the bar turned and said, 'G'day Don. Good to see you.' It was the worst shock of my life. I thought I was looking at a ghost. It was the man we had left behind after Bardia, covered in a blanket, because we thought he had been killed in the shelling.

He explained over a couple of beers that one shell had stunned him, knocking the wind out of him. While he was lying there on the ground, he could hear us arguing about dragging him in. He said he couldn't speak, or cry out to us, but could hear every word we said. He remembered me because I had argued the strongest for going over the top and bringing him into our bunker, when everyone else said it was too late and too risky. He said it was the next shell that did the damage, blowing off an arm and a leg, and ripping out half his stomach. 'If the boys had listened to you, Don, I'd still be in one piece,' he said.

Melbourne was full of surprises. I was hurrying along the platform at Spencer Street Station one day, not long after my return to Australia, when a voice called out loud and clear behind me: 'Don Watt! Don Watt!' I turned around and there was this fellow with a look about him that meant trouble. 'Don Watt,' he said. 'You tried to kill me in Greece, but I got home and I wasn't taken POW like you.'

He climbed onto the train and sat down near me. I was able to have a good look at him and recognised him as a soldier who had climbed into my foxhole in Greece. And as for me trying to kill him, as he was telling all and sundry, he had damn near killed me and a dozen other blokes when he started to crack under the constant German bombardment. He became such a menace — to himself and to the rest of us — that Sol Bercove, the other bloke I was sharing the trench with, and I kept banging him on the head with a tin hat to knock him out.

We were pinned down in our trench for nearly five days, unable to move because of the German onslaught, and what with all the noise of the bombing, the machine-gun attacks, the air-raid sirens and the howling of the Stuka bombers overhead, the man was going off his rocker, getting more and more panicked and wanting to climb out of the trench. It was a cruel thing to do, to keep whacking him on the head, but Sol reckoned that's what they did during World War I. And besides, his behaviour was threatening our lives. We had taken him to the doctor a few days earlier, but there was nothing he could do for him. And now here he was, on a packed train leaving Melbourne, saying I'd tried to kill him! I thought at first he might have been joking with his comments, but he wasn't. In his mind I'd tried to do him in, and he kept on about it. It became really embarrassing.

The weeks continued to fly by, with me going for more medical check-ups to Melbourne, where they tried to patch up my wartime injuries. My nose was so badly broken that it had to be pierced on both sides to allow the air to get through. The operation wasn't as successful as the doctors (and I) had hoped, and two months later I had to have it done again. I also made a few trips to Bendigo to see Doris Johns, the woman I was going to marry. Doris was the brother of Horrie Johns, one of my great mates from my larrikin days before the war. We had a lot of catching up to do, Doris and I, and these were dear, sweet times.

It was also wonderful to hear some pithy Australian humour again, too. I was once on a Melbourne tram, when a rather large woman climbed on, loaded up with paper bags of fruit. The tram was so full that it was impossible for any man to get up and offer her his seat, but we could all see that she was having trouble with the paper bags. Sure enough, after a couple of stops, one of the bags burst and oranges fell to the floor, rolling everywhere. Just as the woman bent down to pick them up, she broke wind somewhat noisily.

Quick as a flash, a little old man who was sitting a few

seats away piped up, saying, 'That's right, madam. If you can't catch them, shoot them.' Everyone roared with laughter and the poor woman, terribly embarrassed, got off at the next stop without her oranges. I knew then that I was back in Australia.

On 27 September 1945, I was discharged.

CHAPTER 9
Pubs, Pranks, Police

While I was thrilled to be back in Australia, catching up with my old mates and not having to wear a uniform any more, I was also beginning to realise that it was time to settle down and get a job. I also giving a bit of thought to getting married. After all, I was 27 now, and I wanted to start making my way in the world. As it happened, all three ambitions — getting married, settling down and getting a job — were fulfilled in a single stroke.

One of the first trips I made was to Bendigo, to see my old sweetheart, Doris Johns. Jack Johns, her father, was running a pub just outside town and needed a bit of help. He asked if I'd give him a hand for a few weeks, working behind the bar, pulling and pushing the barrels around in the cellar and generally making myself useful. I was happy to muck in, and I liked the life so much I took to it like a duck to water. Before long, I had the idea of becoming a publican, too.

I've always been a gregarious sort of bloke, and pub life has always appealed to me. I like the convivial atmosphere of a good pub, the natural mateyness that you find in them, the easy friendships you can strike up and the total sense of equality that prevails. A good pub to me isn't just a place where you go for a drink. It's a way of life and an integral part of Australian culture. To me, a good pub is where you can go for a few pots, or middies, after work, have a yarn to friends, and then go home feeling contented and relaxed. A good pub is also a place where, if something is getting you down, say work, or a row you've had with the wife, you will always find a sympathetic ear. You can get a few problems off your chest, with no-one thinking any the less of you.

While there was no denying that running a pub was very hard work, with long hours and plenty on the physical side, it struck me as not being a job so much as a vocation. So, once the idea of running a pub had formed in my mind, it wasn't long before I was giving serious consideration to getting my own licence, and my own pub. With Jack Johns coming along to give professional advice, I travelled the length and breadth of Victoria, looking at one hotel after another, and eventually decided on the Hibernian Hotel at Golden Square, a suburb of Bendigo, which was just a few miles down the road from Jack's pub.

You had to be married to get a hotel licence in Victoria in those days, so until Doris and I named the date, I arranged for her sister to be the manager of the Hibernian. I then applied to the Licensing Court for a licence, knowing it would take a few months for the paperwork to be processed and for the application to go through. As anyone who has been down this path will tell you, getting a hotel licence is no easy matter. It never has been and never will be, and that's probably no bad thing. But in those days, back in late 1945, the Licensing Court could not have been tougher if it was a branch of the Spanish Inquisition. There wasn't a single aspect of my life that they didn't want to know about, and in every detail. Finally, after months of waiting, the day for the hearing arrived. My application was the first on the list and it took the whole day to hear it.

The bench consisted of three magistrates, but it was the leading magistrate, a Mr Campton, who gave me a really hard time. A real tin god, he sat on the bench, pontificating away on the evils of drink and saying what a responsibility hotel owners owed to the community. He then started on me. Getting very personal, he claimed I could not possibly have

enough finance behind me to take on a hotel and, if I did
have the money, I had probably come by it through question-
able means. He then tried to make out that I was just a stooge
for Doris' sister, who had held a hotel licence before the war
and had lost it after a couple of convictions for trading after
hours. In other words, so far as Mr Campton was concerned,
I was just the front man, and Doris' sister was using me as a
back door to get into the hotel trade again.

Well, this made my blood boil. I told the magistrate that
nothing could be further from the truth. I told him I was an
honest man, that I had no criminal convictions whatsoever,
and that what he was suggesting was totally repugnant to me.
I said I had no idea my future sister-in-law had once held a
licence, or had any convictions against her, and that she would
be running the Hibernian strictly as a temporary manager
until Doris and I were married and could move in to run the
pub on a full-time basis. As for finance, I produced my bank
book and explained that I had a fair bit of money behind me
as I had been a POW for four years. I told him my army pay
had built up very nicely because I hadn't had much opportunity to spend it.

I'd been told that one of the other magistrates on the
bench had been in the forces and was sympathetic towards
servicemen, so I put the question to him directly. 'Sir,' I said,
'as a former serviceman yourself, wouldn't you agree that even
a corporal in the army would be able to save enough money
to buy a pub, especially if he had been a POW for four years
and had nothing to spend his money on?' There was silence
in the court and a small smile spread across the magistrate's
face. He knew I was trying to split the bench, to get him on
my side, even if Mr Campton, the senior magistrate, was
against me, and after a few seconds he replied, 'In those circumstances, yes, it is possible.'

Campton was cornered. There was no way now that he
could refuse my application. But he was a vindictive old
bastard who relished his small amount of power, and he was
determined to show who was boss, no matter what it took.

'Very well,' he barked, 'but you'll have to get married

within six weeks.' I couldn't believe it. 'What's the old coot up to now?' I wondered. 'I'm not having this. I'm not copping him telling me what to do!' That old bugger had been against me right from the start and now that he was beaten and had to give me a licence, he was trying to dictate my private life. I was so ropable, I ignored my solicitor and jumped to my feet.

'Excuse me, your Worship,' I said. 'If you don't mind me saying so, I regard my marriage as very much my business — my personal business. I know you are a very important person when it comes to hotels and licensing, but neither you nor anyone else in this world is going to tell me when I'm to get married. How would you like it if you were in my position and I was telling you when to get married?'

I thought he'd have apoplexy. He went so red, I thought he was going to burst. The court went dead quiet — you could have heard a pin drop — and all eyes were on him. Apparently, he ruled the court with a rod of iron, a real martinet, wrapped up in his own importance, and no one had dared take him on this way before. But he knew I was totally within my rights and that he had exceeded his authority. He made a big show of inspecting the papers in front of him and, eventually, grudgingly, he said, 'Licence granted.' I was a happy man.

Other solicitors and applicants in the court were so amazed by what had happened, with someone finally standing up to Mr Campton, that they all crowded round to congratulate me. Someone suggested a drink, and we all popped out to the pub just around the corner from the court, where I was the man of the moment and everyone bought me a drink. I thought that was a very good way to start my career as a hotelier, with other people buying me drinks.

When Doris and I set the date for our marriage, in May 1946, I thought of sending old Campton an invitation, but I didn't want to push my luck.

I stayed at the Hibernian for just on 12 months, learning all the time about what it took to make a good pub and how to get on with the regulars, until the owner decided to sell the freehold. Then, with the money he repaid me on the lease I had bought, I took a lease on the Bridge Hotel, in Castlemaine, with my brother-in-law and old friend Horrie Johns as a partner. These were happy days, with a good crowd of regular drinkers coming to the hotel, and the occasional fun and games with the police, who were always on the lookout for licensees who traded after hours. There were, I must say, a number of times when I thought the entire Victoria Police Force had nothing better to do than breathe down publicans' necks, but then there probably isn't a pub owner anywhere in Australia who hasn't felt that way at some time.

Those were the days when Victorian pubs weren't allowed to open on Sundays, but plenty of publicans were happy to turn a blind eye to the law. If they knew their customers, they would allow a group of regulars in on the quiet, just so long as the police didn't find out. I was very much in this category and had about 20 regulars who came in for a quiet drink of a Sunday morning, even though it was against the law. We had a simple but effective plan worked out in case the police came knocking, and that was just as well. The plan was that while I walked slowly to the door and opened it to the police, grumbling all the time about being disturbed on a Sunday, they would quickly file around behind the bar and go down through the trapdoor and into the cellar. They would then quietly walk across to the other side of the cellar and climb up into the street through the trapdoor where the beer was delivered.

It was a good plan, and any pub that traded on a Sunday needed such a contingency arrangement. After all, you never knew whether the police would come or not. Sometimes they would visit every pub on a single Sunday, and at other times none at all. Sometimes they would just pick on one or two pubs at random. You never knew when they were going to strike and, if you were doing a bit of after-hours trading, you really had to be awake. Well, one Sunday the police did come knocking on the door and the plan went into action. While I slowly went over to the door, calling out, 'All right, all right.

I'm coming. Keep your pants on,' the men nipped round behind the bar and started getting out. By the time the sergeant walked in the bar was empty, but he was very suspicious, mainly because of all the pipe and cigarette smoke.

'How come it's so smoky in here?' he asked.

I looked him straight in the eye. 'It's from last night, mate. I'd have opened the doors and windows to let some fresh air in, but it's illegal for a hotel to open up on a Sunday. If I did you'd come around and charge me.'

I could tell he didn't believe me.

'Don't give me that flannel!' he said. 'Don't get smart with me. We've been keeping our eye on you, Don Watt. You've been trading after hours and we know it. I'll have you for that. I'll have your licence.'

'Don't be daft,' I replied. 'D'you think I'd be so stupid? I wouldn't risk my livelihood that way. For a few lousy beers of a Sunday? Wake up. You've never had any trouble with me before. Take a look yourself. Go on, search the place.'

So he did. He looked around, checking everywhere, even in the cellar, but there was no-one on the premises and no sign of drinking, so he just muttered something and went on his way.

Next day, all the regulars were in the hotel after work as usual. I asked how the escape plan had gone. Well, did they have a story for me. It seems the plan was going like clock-work until one of the men, old Charlie, a fellow in his late 70s, was about to climb from the cellar up into the street, when the man in front of him dropped the trapdoor on him, whacking Charlie on the head, taking the wind out of him and knocking him right back into the cellar. The blokes behind him had to half drag, half carry him up the ladder and out into the street, not daring to utter a sound in case the sergeant heard them and came bolting down. The game would have been well and truly up.

Well, not much happened in small towns in those days, and before long word of the scam was all over town. My little escapade was big news and Charlie was something of a celebrity. But it wasn't long before the police heard about it, too, and they were after my scalp. Accompanied by a constable, the sergeant paid me another visit and read me the riot act for about ten minutes, warning me not to try it again or my licence would be on the line.

Those were the days of the 'six o'clock swill', when people would come in for a drink after work and usually try to get as many pots inside them as they could before the compulsory six o'clock closing time. In those days it was against the law to serve drinks after hours, even to people who were staying in the hotel, but again, many hoteliers took a sporting chance. On one occasion, two commercial travellers, or sales reps as they call them today, were staying in the hotel and having a quiet drink after hours, when there was a sudden ratt-tatt-tatt on the door. Only the police knocked on a door that way, so I quickly told the men to go through to my bedroom and hide there until I gave them the OK.

This was, generally speaking, a wise and safe thing to do because, although the police could inspect the public areas of a hotel, they needed a warrant to search the private rooms, and there was no way they would have a warrant with them on a strictly routine visit. As it happens, on this occasion it was a false alarm — it was only one of the regulars coming back to collect the lunch bag that he'd left behind — so I went along to the bedroom and told the men that it was safe to come out.

As they came out, I noticed one of them was wearing a light-grey suit, which I didn't think he'd been wearing before, but I thought no more of it until a couple of days later, when he came back to the hotel and gave me a parcel. It contained my grey suit, freshly dry-cleaned. 'I dived under your bed and hit the bedpan,' he explained. 'There was disinfectant in the pan and it went all over my clothes.'

I told him he was lucky it was only disinfectant.

Then there was the time one of the regulars called in for a drink after hours while waiting for his uncle who lived next door. It was his bad luck that he had just started on his second or third pot, when the police knocked on the door for a routine inspection. I let him out of the side door and into the yard, before letting in the constable, who also went out through the side door. I thought the regular would have been well out of it by then, but no way. He'd tried to climb through a hole in the side fence, but the copper saw his big behind poking out and gave it a darned good kick. We all laughed so much that the policeman did nothing about this infringement of the law and let us all off with a warning.

It was at the Bridge Hotel that I had the idea of getting a hotel cat. It was an immediate hit with the regulars, but it soon developed a taste for beer. I'm not too sure how it happened, but I think someone must have put an ashtray full of beer on the ground, and the cat had a few licks, then a few more licks, until I had a boozing cat on my hands. This didn't bother me too much, but the cat became a real dipsomaniac, drinking from the drip tray and getting so drunk it passed out under people's feet. I locked it out after a while, but it always sneaked back in. It was then so desperate for a drink that it would leap up onto the bar and drink from people's glasses. That was the last straw.

I loved the hotel trade, and Castlemaine was a beaut little town, but owing to a combination of circumstances, things weren't going right. After 12 months or so, my knee was playing up, as was my back, and my nerves were in a shocking state. I don't want to dwell on it, but my marriage had also hit a rocky patch. I had lost a lot of weight through worrying about one thing and another, and the doctor reckoned there was nothing he could do for me except to recommend I give up the pub and try working outdoors for a while. I didn't like the sound of that, as being a publican means you're your own boss, but the doc said I had no choice. And I was lucky that I had a trade to fall back on.

When I was a lad, I had picked up a bit of carpentry from Dad, so I went into the building trade, working as a carpenter for various firms, and ending up as a foreman on a few country constructions, including a million-pound extension to the Shepparton Packing Company. At one stage, I even teamed up with Dad, who was getting on by then, of course, and the two of us worked on one of the first new housing estates being developed by A.V. Jennings at Seymour, near my old army-training camp at Puckapunyal.

I was a bit worried at first that I didn't have a carpenter's ticket, so I asked a mate who worked for the BWIU — the Building Workers' Industrial Union — what the situation was, as I didn't want to cause any trouble. 'D'you reckon I should take a trade test so I can get my carpenter's ticket?' I asked. He just shrugged his shoulders. 'Don,' he said, 'you're one of the best carpenters I know. I reckon you'd fly through the test in about two minutes, but I can't see the need. You're recognised as a qualified tradesman. I'll square it with the blokes on the site and if there's any trouble I'll let you know.' I'm glad he was such a good mate. The BWIU was fairly peaceful in those days and didn't pull the huge strikes that they did in later years. But I'm glad I spoke to them and did the right thing. The last thing I wanted was to be caught up in the middle of a strike and accused of being a blackleg, or of scabbing.

It wasn't a bad life, working as a carpenter in the building trade, and the money was good on the big construction sites. However, I soon got tired of working away from home and went back to Bendigo, where I built houses for while and worked on some new developments, including the new high school, the technical college and the teachers' college. Then my back started giving me real trouble and, after a couple of years, I decided to go back to hotels.

I drove to Melbourne to talk to a hotel broker, but although he had several pubs on his books, there wasn't one that interested me. I was on the point of leaving, feeling very depressed, when he mentioned, quite out of the blue, that the Railway Hotel at Castlemaine was on the market. I jumped at it.

'The Railway?' I said. 'I know the Railway Hotel. It's a great little pub. That's the one for me!' The broker was so surprised he couldn't believe what I was saying.

'It's only a small hotel, Don,' he said. 'I only mentioned it in passing. It wasn't a serious suggestion. Mate, it sells barely three 18-gallon kegs of beer a week. No-one can make a living out of that. You'll go bust in no time. That's why the owner's selling up and moving on. He can't get out fast enough. That's why the pub's on the market. It's not for you mate. You're a friend and I can't do it to you. No way. I don't even want to show it to you.'

'Listen,' I said. 'I know Castlemaine. I worked there a few years ago, running the Bridge Hotel. And do you want to know something? All the time I was running the Bridge, I had my eye on the Railway. I reckon it's the best pub in town. I've been after it for years. Don't bother to show it to me, I know exactly what it's like. I'll take it! And, as you tell me it's such a lousy pub, I don't expect to pay over the odds for it. I expect to get it at a rock-bottom price!'

It was 1964, and I was aged 46.

As you would expect, the Railway Hotel was opposite the railway station. It was also opposite the football ground and had plenty of parking. Although we still had six o'clock closing, licensing hours were about to be extended to ten o'clock and I thought the big car park would be a drawcard. I was right. Licensing hours were extended and, with cars becoming more and more popular, it wasn't long before I had built up a very good business. There were never any fights and whenever one looked like starting, I would quickly tell the instigators that there were other pubs they could drink in.

It was also a very happy pub, and the regulars always rallied round when I decided to do a bit of fund-raising, such as for the local football club or for the fire brigade. One fund-raiser that always had the money rolling in was when, because of my name, I banned the use of the word 'what'. Anyone who said 'what' had to put 20 cents into a jar. You know, it's amazing how often people say 'What?' I raised about $200 for the local hospital that way. We were all very pleased.

As a hotelier, you had to be alert to trouble and make

sure none ever came your way. For the most part, I'm proud of my record of hardly ever having any trouble with hoons on the premises. But trouble certainly seemed on the cards one Saturday afternoon, when Castlemaine was invaded by a bikie gang. There was a brewery strike throughout Victoria at the time, and Slim Dusty's song, 'The Pub with No Beer', was on all the radio stations. Because beer was short, various gangs of Hell's Angels would ride around the countryside and pick on whatever town and pub took their fancy. While some pubs had run out of beer altogether, others had a few kegs in reserve and were rationing it among their regulars. These were the pubs the bikie gangs liked to find, so they could stir up trouble.

As soon as the bikie gang rode in, the fellow who ran the hotel on that side of town played cockatoo, and phoned all the other publicans so they would be awake to what was going on. On this occasion, there were about 30 bikies and they had split into different groups. It was only a matter of time before a group of about ten of them pulled up outside the Railway, exhausts blasting and leather jackets gleaming menacingly in the sunlight. I went out the front door and started chatting to them, saying I was very sorry but I'd run dry days ago.

They were very polite and civil — strangely polite and civil, considering all the horror stories about bikie gangs that I'd heard. Thanking me, they rode off, all except for one bloke who waited until the others had ridden off up the road, and then called my bluff and came in. He seemed a nice enough chap, so I served him a pot and we started chatting. Well, you could have knocked me down with a feather. He told me that the bikies weren't the usual long-haired rowdies looking for trouble, but a group of lawyers, doctors and businessmen who had formed a motor cycle club at university and who still got together now and again for a ride into the countryside. Six weeks later, 20 of them came back to the Railway Hotel and had a good time mixing with the regulars. They said I had been so convincing when I told them I had no beer, that they had believed me immediately. There was no way they were going to let me live it down.

I was at the Railway Hotel for ten years, and pretty well enjoyed every second of it. I completely revamped the interior, pulling out walls and extending the bar area, giving the place much more of a club atmosphere than most pubs in the area. I'm happy to say that my customers liked it, too, and I built up a very good business. Most of the local businessmen drank at the Railway, and reckoned it was the only pub in Castlemaine that was worth going to. They also helped me 'police' the place. They appreciated the firm hand I took with potential trouble-makers, telling them to leave and not mincing my words, and before long my regulars were doing all that work for me. If anyone became rowdy or it looked as though a fight was going to break out, they would walk over and say, 'Come on, this is a nice pub. There's plenty of other pubs if you want to behave that way. You're not welcome here.'

I had a few run-ins with the police, for trading after hours, of course. On one occasion, it was touch and go, all because of some miserable old woman who lived in the house next door. A lane ran down the side of the pub, and one of the pub's ground-floor windows looked out onto it. This was all very useful for after-hours trading, and I was in the habit of taking the money off people in the bar and serving their bottles through the side window, where we wouldn't be seen. This proved to be very handy indeed until one night one of the regulars smashed his car into the garage of the woman next door, and she started screaming blue bloody murder.

The police came zooming up in a patrol car and, without even asking any questions, started accusing me of after-hours trading.

'What a flaming liberty!' I said.

'Don't give us that, Don Watt,' they replied. 'We've had our eye on you. We've been waiting for something like this and now we've gotcha!'

'Officer,' I replied. 'This has absolutely nothing to do with me. Joe here,' I said, pointing to the man who had bashed into the garage, 'had a few drinks here this evening, sure. But he told me he skidded on the gravel. Why don't you ask the woman next door. I'm sure she saw everything.'

Well, the old woman hadn't seen a thing, of course. And keeping a straight face and not allowing himself to be ruffled, Joe backed up every word I said. The police had to drop the matter. They didn't like it, I can tell you. I might add that it took years to hose down the old woman. Every night from then on, she seemed to be watching her clock and peeping out from behind the curtains to see if I was flouting the law.

On another occasion, I wasn't so lucky. Because I ran a good pub, with clean accommodation, and right across the road from the railway, all the commercial travellers used to stay with me. Naturally, being guests in the hotel, they were able to drink after hours, and there were no problems there. In fact, Victoria's licensing laws were relaxing a tad, and I'd had a phone call from a mate of mine in Melbourne to tell me that guests in the hotel could now take alcohol off licensed premises with them, if, say, they were going to a restaurant or to a friend's place for dinner.

I spread the word about this to all the travellers, and they were delighted to hear about it. But one night, just as one of the travellers legged it out of the door with a couple of bottles under his arm, this copper, a senior constable — and a really nasty piece of work — leapt out of nowhere.

'Gotcha!' he said. 'You know it's against the law for people to take grog off licensed premises. We've all been watching you, Watt, and now I've got you cold.'

I tried explaining there had been a change in the law, and that he should know about it, and that just made him madder.

'Don't tell me my job, Watt,' he said. 'I'm the law around here, not you. So don't get smart. No-one has told me anything about a change in the licensing law, and I'm charging you. OK?'

Well, the copper made a case against me and it went to court. I had to get a barrister up from Melbourne to represent me. The case didn't take long. The barrister simply produced a copy of the *Government Gazette* with the details of the change of law and it was all over. The magistrate was furious — not with me, but with the copper, and gave him a right dressing-down about wasting people's time and money. 'I know this is a small town,' he said, 'but I don't think it's too much to expect the police to know the law they're supposed to be enforcing.'

The copper was really dirty about it. He was clearly after promotion, and he spent the next three months outside my pub, night after night, making sure everyone was off the premises by 10 p.m. Thankfully, neither my customers nor I were able to oblige him with even the smallest infringement.

He was transferred to Melbourne a couple of months later and promoted to sergeant. So far as I was concerned, it was good riddance and I hoped I'd seen the last of him. It wasn't. He wandered into The Railway a few years later, wearing civvies. He said he had retired from the force and had moved back to Castlemaine because he liked the town so much.

'I reckon you should buy me a beer for old times' sake,' he said, bold as brass.

'Mate,' I said. 'I wouldn't buy you a beer if it was a penny a pot!'

'What's the matter with you then?' he said, very much taken aback. 'There's no reason to be like that. I'm only trying to be friendly.'

I then told him the whole story — he had forgotten it — about the traveller with the couple of bottles, and the trouble he had put me to when I was in the right all along.

Well, I shamed him. He walked out of the pub looking absolutely stupid. And that was the last I saw of him.

The time I spent at The Railway should have been ten of the happiest years of my life. However, towards the end, I had marriage problems all over again, ending in divorce. In addition to that, my knee was now giving me so much trouble, the doctors were talking about taking the leg off. What with all the worry, my health went down alarmingly. A few mates told me that, because I was still suffering from a war injury, I was entitled to compensation as a returned serviceman. I had several sessions with the Veterans' Review Board to see what could be done, and I was eventually awarded a 40 per cent disability allowance.

It was at this time that I decided, for one reason or another, that I needed a complete change. I needed to move away from Victoria, put the past behind me and find a new, fresh field. My marriage was over and, sadly, I didn't have any children to consider — my cousin Ron carried on the Watt family name. I bought a Franklyn caravan, complete with shower, and set out to find peace on my own, fishing on the Murray River, out Echuca way.

I moved around a bit over the next few years, going to Kyneton to help a friend, Les (Doc) Keating, get established in a hotel, then to Brisbane, where I ran a snack bar at Stone's Corner, before returning to Castlemaine, where I worked as a carpenter again, building new wards for old folk at the Alexandra Hospital. While I was working there, a steel scaffold collapsed under me and I fell onto the corner of a plywood form used for boxing concrete. The wood penetrated my stomach, caused a hernia, and aggravated my back problem. Not for the first time in my life, I was in a terrible state.

It was a year before my health started to improve and I was able to go on a bit of a holiday, fishing along the Murray with a few mates. One really hot day, with the mercury around 40 degrees Celsius, I was having a swim, when I suddenly had severe pains in my chest and couldn't breathe. This happened a couple of times, so I finally went to hospital for an ECG, but the doctors couldn't find anything wrong. I was still in pain from time to time and it was only when I was examined by a young doctor, recently qualified and with two years' experience in a heart clinic, that I discovered what the problem was. My heart was in such a bad state that I needed a bypass operation.

This was carried out successfully, I'm pleased to say, but there were a few unexpected side effects — I'd come to expect this, with my health. If it wasn't one thing, it was something else. This time I had golden staph of the knee. They had removed a vein from my knee to be used in the heart operation, and now my knee was infected, and the infection was spreading. Apparently, some clips used when the vein was removed had come adrift and not been taken out. I had a talk with an old nursing sister, who said the best thing I could do was lie in the sun for a while. I thought, 'Why not?'. I packed my caravan and headed north.

CHAPTER 10
Joan

There's an old song that says something about love being lovelier the second time around. In my case I know it's true, because in my second wife, Joan, I have found a true soulmate. To me, a wife is someone you want to be with all the time, each and every day, someone you can confide in, someone you trust, someone who will always be there for you, someone to share life's experiences with, to cheer you up when you're down and laugh with you when you're happy. Of course, being a husband means the same thing; it carries the same duties and responsibilities. My only regret where Joan is concerned, is that I didn't meet her years earlier.

After driving north for the second or third time and running a few small businesses in one town or another, I pulled in with my caravan to the Billabong Caravan Park in Tweed Heads. It was clean, orderly and well maintained and, although there was nothing special about the place, it suited me down to the ground. It was just the spot to pull in for a couple of weeks and let my health recover. There, I could figure out what I was going to do with the rest of my life, while enjoying what seemed to me to be an absolutely perfect climate. The year was 1981 and I was aged 63.

I had been at the Billabong for about a week, minding my own business, taking in the scenery, going for walks along

the beach and generally taking stock of my life, when I came
out of the shower block one Sunday morning and noticed a
nice-looking caravan with a *For Sale* sign next to it. It was
either the van that was for sale or the tubs of flowers the sign
was sitting on, so, in my usual direct and cheeky way, I thought
I'd find out which. I had been thinking about getting a new
caravan, because mine was proving rather small as a permanent
home. This one was about ten metres (30 feet) long and had
a large annexe. It seemed ideal.

Wearing a pair of shorts and thongs, and still with the
towel around my head from the shower, I knocked on the
door. A good-looking woman answered.

'Hello,' I said. 'What's for sale? The van, the flowers, or
what?'

The woman looked at me as if to say, 'Who's this cheeky
customer?' and invited me in to look around.

'Excuse the mess,' she said, waving her arm at a whole
lot of furniture that was cluttering up the place. 'I've just moved
out of my flat and I'm still deciding which bits of furniture to
hang on to. That's the reason I'm selling. It's a nice van, nothing
wrong with it at all. But I've got all this furniture and even
after I sell a few pieces, I'll still need something bigger.'

Well, she wasn't wrong about the van being too small. It
was considerably bigger than mine, but still wasn't big enough
for what I had in mind. I told her I was sorry I'd wasted her
time. We chatted on for a while, talking about caravan life,
the advantages and the drawbacks, and whether you were
really that much better off than living in a house or a flat, and
I kept thinking, 'Gee, she's a nice woman. I can really talk to
her. She's beaut.'

I was just about to go, when the woman, who had
introduced herself as Joan Peterson, asked if I was there on
my own.

'All alone,' I said. 'Just me.'

She looked me up and down and said, 'I'm only asking
because I've got two tickets for Phyllis Diller at the Twin Towns
Club next Sunday. Would you like to come with me?

'Oh, yes,' I said. 'That sounds good. All right.'

So, it was a date.

Well, I hardly set eyes on Joan for the rest of that week. I mean, I'd see her in her van, talking or reading or having a cup of coffee, but somehow I never went over to talk to her, even though we were going out together in a few days' time. I suppose I didn't want to seem pushy. And I certainly didn't want to intrude.

Anyway, Sunday evening came around, so I put on a clean shirt and tie and knocked on her door. We went to the Twin Towns, had dinner and a couple of drinks and really enjoyed the show. I dropped her back at her caravan later that evening, and shook hands with her.

'Thank you for the show,' I said. 'I really enjoyed it. It's nice to have a night out for a change.'

She smiled and said, 'Oh, that's all right. I enjoyed it, too.'

I felt I wanted to see her again and was wondering how to go about it. Then she beat me to it.

'Oh, by the way,' she said, as I walked her to the caravan door. 'I've got two more tickets for next Sunday's show, if you'd like to go.'

'Fine. Love to,' I said with a smile. So I knew she quite liked me.

That was it for another week. Same as before, I didn't see her during the week, but called for her on the Sunday evening, and we had another pleasant time. We talked a lot more this time, and I told her a bit about myself: about my life running hotels and things like that (nothing about the concentration camp). In turn, she told me about herself: how she had been divorced for 20 years and about her four children, including the former Australian champion surfer Michael Peterson, and Tom Peterson, another good surfer.

It was all very enjoyable and, as I dropped Joan back at her caravan later that night and shook hands and thanked her again, I was really thinking to myself what a top woman she was. She had a good figure in those days too, very trim. A few days later, Joan came over to my caravan. She was taking her new car into the garage for a service and wondered if I would follow her in my car and give her a lift back. Well, what gentleman wouldn't?

We were driving past a caravan park on the way back when Joan said, 'Hey, Don. D'you see that place there, that caravan park? I was born there in a bag-hut years ago when it was just a paddock. It was a lovely place then.'

'Oh, really?' I said. 'Well, it still looks very nice.'

'Ah, it was really lovely in those days,' she said. 'The grass used to shine in the sun. And there were some really beautiful trees. Y'know, I have such wonderful memories of that place. Every time I drive along this way I think of my childhood and how happy I was in that paddock.

'In fact, I made a promise to myself years and years ago. I told myself that if ever I get married again, that's where it will be.'

'I'll marry you,' I said, without thinking about it for a second.

Joan thought about it for a minute and said, 'Yes. Yes, all right.'

Joan was 49, 14 years younger than me, but I knew she was the woman I had been looking for. The age difference didn't seem to bother her and it certainly didn't bother me. We were married on 27 September, the anniversary of my discharge from the army.

The reason I'm writing about Joan so much is because without her I would not have been able to face, and overcome, the horrors of the past. Joan is one in a million, a woman with a big heart and a ton of compassion and understanding. She is also a very humane and very sensible person. She has her feet on the ground, and this is important to me.

Since that time in November 1987, when I found myself saying, 'I was there, too,' after seeing the item in the newspaper about the Veterans' Affairs Department looking for ex-servicemen who had been imprisoned in Nazi concentration camps, Joan has been behind me every step of the way. She has helped me confront the memories of Auschwitz and overcome them by learning to live with them. It was also her idea that I should write these memoirs: not out of vanity, but as a means of confronting the past.

It was Joan's idea that I write to Canberra. She nagged me into it. Well, 'nag' is probably too strong a word, but she certainly kept on at me to do something. So, with Joan's encouragement, on 14 February 1988, I wrote to the Concentration Camps Committee, telling them I had been in Belsen and Auschwitz. They wrote back some few weeks later saying they had no record of me having been in a concentration camp. Well, there wouldn't be, because I hadn't told anyone about it until then. And, in the silliest line I have read in my life, they wanted to know if I 'had any witnesses.' What did they mean 'any witnesses'? You could tell the letter had been written by a bureaucrat who had never set foot outside Canberra. What did they think I was doing in Auschwitz? Wandering around with a notebook and pencil writing down names and addresses? I was so angry, I wrote back saying, 'You ask if I had any witnesses. Well, I stood in the middle of the camp and yelled out that I was going to escape.' That would have put a flea in someone's ear, that's for sure.

It seems my application for compensation caused a bit of head-scratching in Canberra. The Veterans' Affairs Department could find no reference, in my service record or in their departmental records, of my having been in a concentration camp. They wrote to the International Committee of the Red Cross, in Geneva, who passed the letter to the Red Cross International Tracing Service, in Arolsen, Germany, which holds the records of approximately 13.5 million people who were persecuted by the Third Reich, including being incarcerated in concentration camps. Because of the huge number of requests for information from all around the world, it took eight months for the Red Cross to confirm my story.

After that initial response to the newspaper article, of me saying, 'I was there too,' my health went down alarmingly.

After a few months, I developed very bad diarrhoea and was going to the toilet 20 to 30 times a day. Doctors checked me out, but could find nothing wrong with me, of course. It was all in the mind, only I didn't know it at the time, and neither did they.

Nearly two years later, in December 1989, I had the first of two minor strokes which, I have since been told, were also triggered by the mental anguish I was suffering. I spent two weeks in Greenslopes Repatriation Hospital, in Brisbane, and I cannot thank the people there enough for their care and kindness. By now I was thinking about Auschwitz and Belsen a great deal, and the diarrhoea was worse than ever. The doctors said I had dysentery, but they still couldn't find the cause.

A month after this, I had a letter from the Veterans' Affairs Department in Canberra, telling me that Rear-Admiral Neil Ralph, chairman of the Concentration Camps Committee, would be calling on me at home to interview me about my time in the concentration camps. That was the moment I had dreaded, having to open my mind again to all the atrocities. Admiral Ralph knew about Auschwitz. He had seen films of the place, that had been confiscated by the Allies, and had heard what had happened through other interviews with POWs.

He asked me about the conditions I had lived in, the type of work that was done in the camp, the position of various buildings, and the colour of the SS uniforms. They were very specific questions, designed to elicit information that you wouldn't be able to read in books, see in the movies, or learn from someone else. He was after the sort of information that only someone who had actually been in Auschwitz would know about.

He asked me to draw a plan of the place, showing the location of the various huts, the gas chambers and the crematoria. He also wanted me to tell him something about what had happened 'on the other side' — at the Auschwitz concentration camp. I remember my reply: 'I can't tell you about that, sir. I wasn't allowed over there. I was in Auschwitz–

Birkenau, the death camp. I wasn't allowed into the con-centration camp part and never went there, so I can't tell you anything about it.' I don't know if he was sounding me out, or what.

Admiral Ralph was very understanding and sympathetic. The interview lasted a couple of hours. Joan sat in with us and couldn't believe the things I was saying. Towards the end, I broke down and cried. For a week after that, I couldn't talk to anyone without breaking down. I was in a terrible state.

Within two weeks of talking to Admiral Ralph, the diarrhoea started to ease and within a month it had gone. So far as I am concerned, writing the letter in 1988 brought to the surface everything I had been suppressing for more than 40 years. Talking about it was my way of handling it. If I had talked about it when I returned from the war, and got it off my chest as quickly as possible, I wouldn't have suffered the mental anguish that I was now going through.

I told the doctors about this on a subsequent visit to Greenslopes, when the old war wound in my knee started playing up again. The knee had never really been the same since being sliced by that lump of shrapnel during the Battle for Crete. It was now giving me so much trouble, that the doctors were again talking openly and seriously about taking the leg off. I objected to that very strongly, and eventually they fitted me with an artificial knee which can bend to 60 degrees. This has helped me tremendously and also eased the pain.

They're a wonderful team at Greenslopes, doctors, nurses, social workers, administration staff — everyone — and they encouraged me to talk about my overall mental and physical condition. This time I told them about Auschwitz and some of the things I had seen there, about the nightmares I'd been having and the constant diarrhoea. They were genuinely amazed. They said I hadn't seemed the kind of person who suffered psychosomatically.

Finally, in April 1990, I received a cheque for $10,000 from the Department of Veterans' Affairs as compensation for my suffering at Auschwitz. The cheque was accompanied by an official letter from the Concentration Camps Committee, confirming my war-time experiences.

The wheels of bureaucracy turn incredibly slowly. While my application for compensation was being processed, I went through the most awful nightmares, with memory after memory of what I had been through coming rushing back to me. I would lie awake unable to sleep, or wake up screaming in a muck sweat. The nightmares took different forms, but three of them recurred time and again and still come back to haunt me occasionally. One is of me being back in the underground cell at Auschwitz, feeling the rats scurrying along, and hearing them eating the bodies of prisoners who had died in the night. The second is of seeing pile upon pile of gassed bodies waiting to be thrown into the furnace. The third, and possibly the worst nightmare, is of seeing my little Polish mate looking at me with his big, soulful eyes, saying, 'Ossie, Ossie' as the Capos threw him, living, breathing, screaming, into the furnace for not working hard enough.

I don't get the nightmares so often now, and I'm sure that it was Joan's therapy of getting me to write down everything I could remember, that helped bring this about. It cleared my mind and, as a result, I'm more at ease with myself. But even now, when people ask me about the events at Auschwitz and my mind goes to those days on the furnace, I think of my little Polish mate and I cry. The tears well up in my eyes and there is nothing I can do to stop them.

Why is this? Am I, in some way, punishing myself for having done nothing to save the little fellow? I don't know. As I said earlier, I couldn't do anything to save him and, more than that, I would have been killed if I'd tried. For what it's worth, I don't think I'm alone in this. Since word got around that I was writing this book, I have spoken to one or two other concentration-camp survivors who have ghastly recollections of their experiences, too. It's the realisation that they and I survived, while so many thousands, even millions, of others perished, that brings on the tears.

At first I was ashamed of crying. I belong to a generation that has lived with hardship and has learnt to take it as part of life. There was the Depression and then the war, and men accepted these things stoically, uncomplainingly. The last thing any man of my generation would do is cry, no matter what. I now know how silly it is to keep things bottled up. It can affect you physically and mentally — as it has certainly affected me.

In 1990 I found out that Monty McMahon, one of the great mates of my larrikin youth when we rode motor bikes and chased girls around Mildura, was living in Maroochydore, in Queensland, just a couple of hours from Tweed Heads. I called on him out of the blue, then Joan and I started to visit him and his wife every month.

I had seen Monty only briefly after the war and we had so much catching up to do that we talked for three days. Our wives said they had never seen two men talk so much. We had been special mates before the war and, on embarkation leave in March 1940, I had given Monty an army photo of me. He still had it in his wallet, and said how he wished he had joined up with me, because he had missed me so much. We laughed a lot together about the old days and the pranks we had got up to, but I didn't tell him anything about Auschwitz, even though my claim for compensation was being processed by then. Don't ask me why I didn't talk to Monty about it, but somehow it didn't seem appropriate. I didn't want anything spoil the wonderful feeling of yarning away with an old mate about the good times we had together. A few months after our first visit, Monty had a massive cerebral haemorrhage and died.

I lost another special army mate in 1991, when Gordon (Shorty) Gibbs, who'd been with me in Palestine, passed away. One particular pub crawl we went on, while on leave in Tel Aviv, has stayed firmly in my memory. I had already started doing the rounds of the pubs, when Shorty came looking for me, calling into every bar he could think of and having a beer in each of them. By the time he caught up with me, he was as full as a boot and ready to fight the world. This was very silly of Shorty because, well, he was rather short — about 1.7 metres (five foot five).

Anyway, he was determined to have a go at someone, and for some reason he picked on the biggest soldier in the bar. He started abusing him, calling him a big galoot and that sort of thing, and boasting that he could beat him with one hand tied behind his back, no matter how big the soldier was. Well, after a while the big fellow got a bit narky. He was fed up with this little runt of a bloke sledging off at him all the time, so he rolled his sleeves up and the two of them got stuck into each other.

It was a massacre. The big fellow started bashing Shorty all over the place. If another soldier and I hadn't stepped in to break up the fight, I'm quite sure Shorty would have been murdered. He had a black eye, his nose was bloody and a couple of teeth were missing. He was dead on his feet and he didn't know it. 'Oh, boys,' he said. 'I nearly had him. If youse blokes hadn't come along, I'd have made mincemeat of him.' He then passed out cold, and we had to carry him back to the camp.

It was only the next morning, when he saw his face in the mirror, that Shorty realised what had happened to him. 'Gawd, fellas,' he said. 'I must have been as full as a tick. How big did you say the other fella was? Blimey! How could I have been so stupid?' He moderated his drinking after that, and only picked on people his own size. I caught up with Shorty after the war, when I was running The Railway in Castlemaine. He had come to live in Castlemaine and he visited the pub quite regularly for a talk about old times. We also we went to a couple of reunions together and, as time went on, the odd comrade's funeral. We were all getting older.

George Timmis, the Cockney POW I had befriended way back in Stalag 13C, came over from England with his wife, Flo, in December 1993. It's amazing how he got on to me. Barbara Fitzgibbon, who helped me with the first draft of this book, took a photo of George to England, when she went there on holiday, and placed it in various London suburban papers with a small item on how I was trying to find him. Months later, while he was doing casual work at the Royal Mint, a workmate went up to George with a copy of the paper and said, 'Hey, George. This looks like you when you were young.' George saw my name and Barbara's address and was so excited, that he rushed home to get a letter off to me. When he and Flo arrived in Australia, we hadn't seen each other for 49 years. We just talked and talked as if it were yesterday. George said he still had the shorts I'd made him in Hammelburg in 1942, and kept them as a souvenir.

There have been other reunions over the years, most of them wonderful and brought about through snippets of information in the 2/7th Battalion newsletter or in *Barbed Wire*, the official journal for Australian POWs. In January 1981 I received the address of Stan Enks, the soldier with the insatiable sex drive whom I had introduced to the joys of women, when we were based in Palestine. I hadn't seen Stan since 1941, when he caught a bullet in the arm at Bardia. He was now living south of Brisbane and I called in to see him, out of the blue. He was enormously surprised, as he had always wondered what had happened to me. Sadly, Stan was a very sick man by then, but he had one particular thing he wanted to tell me about.

'Don, I have a confession to make,' he said.

'Oh, yes? What's that then?'

'Do you remember that time in Cairo, when you and Don Jones took me to the VD centre because you were so concerned about me?'

'Do I remember! Stan, there was no stopping you!'

'Well, you stopped me all right. Do you remember that after we visited the centre I said I was going to the knocking shop? Well, mate, I was putting you on. You and Don frightened me so much, I didn't touch another woman until I met my wife!'

Stan's wife laughed. 'It's true,' she said. 'He's told me that story a thousand times, about how you introduced him to women and how you turned him off women!'

Stan died in 1982.

Another comrade from the 2/7th whom I particularly enjoyed catching up with was Steve Bernard. I first met Steve after he had finished his officer training at Duntroon and was doing a stint as regimental sergeant major with the 2/7th at Puckapunyal. He was made a lieutenant after that, and I served with him in Palestine. I hadn't seen him since the bayonet charge at Bardia, so we had a lot to talk about. To me, Steve was always a fine man and the model of what an officer should be. He proved his authority on the parade ground and in action, and I am proud to have served under him.

I caught up with Steve in 1991. He had been running his own real-estate business in Orange, NSW, although by the time I met up with him, he had pretty well retired. He told me that he had also been taken POW on Crete. This had brought his military career to an abrupt halt, which was sad because, to my mind, he could have become a colonel or even a brigadier. He said he had been awarded the Military Cross on his return to Australia, and I can't think of a finer soldier to receive such a high decoration.

In many ways, Steve was my idol. We had been on quite a few dangerous missions in the desert, and this had heightened the respect which I knew was mutual. Surprisingly, he had told his children nothing about his army exploits, no matter how much they pleaded with him. You know how children are: they love it when their father tells them stories about himself. The children were quite grown up by then, of course, and leading their own lives. One son, Stephen, was a fast bowler for New South Wales for a few years. Another son, Peter, went to Duntroon, following in his father's footsteps.

We must have yarned on for about three hours. Steve's wife, Dorothy, said she really wished the children had been there to see and hear us. 'Steve has never talked so much about the war,' she said.

But, then, we had been comrades-in-arms, and that's not something a man ever takes lightly. Never has, never will. It's the same with all servicemen, especially those who have been overseas on active service, fighting for what they believe is right, and defending it, literally, to the death. Such men share the worst conditions imaginable, and a bond exists between them that's stronger than any other. You have to have lived it to know it. To some, it's stronger than marriage, stronger than nationhood. That's the way it will always be for the men who have been there and experienced it.

And I, for one, am proud of it.

Postscript

There have been four drafts of this book. The first I started after Rear-Admiral Ralph interviewed me for the Concentration Camps Committee. I wrote and wrote for six or seven hours a day, often in the small hours of the morning when I couldn't sleep. I have to say that I didn't set out to write my life story, or an account of my seven months at Auschwitz, I just needed to get things off my chest and writing seemed a good way of doing it.

It's amazing how one thing leads to another. While I was scribbling away frantically at all hours of the day and night, I had a letter from the Keith Murdoch Sound Archive at the Australian War Memorial in Canberra, asking if they could interview me about my experiences. Of course I was happy to, and an Ed Stokes came to my home and recorded seven and a half hours of interview with me. I later received a friendly letter from Roslyn Russell, the project co-ordinator, thanking me for my help and saying how enthusiastic they were about the quality of my recollections.

Talking to the Sound Archive people brought back more memories, and it was my wife, Joan, who suggested I should add a few stories about my life before and after the war, so that anyone who wanted to read it would have a better picture of me and the sort of person I am, where I came from and what I'm all about. So, with Joan's guidance, I just started at the beginning, from when I was born up to the present day. It took about a year to get the first draft finished. Then, Barbara Fitzgibbon, a former journalist now living in Tweed Heads, helped me knock it into shape.

As a result, I was able to publish a slim A4-sized booklet of my story. It was called *I Was There Too*, and I had 500 copies printed at my expense by a local printer. Thanks to a small article about the book in the *Gold Coast Bulletin*, I sold these for $15 a copy through my Tweed Heads post-office box. Writing that first draft got a load off my mind, and the more I wrote, the more I started to remember. I began updating the *I Was There Too* booklet almost before it was printed.

Soon after the booklet appeared, I had a phone call from a journalist on the *Australasian Post*, who was interested in interviewing me for an article. More memories came back after that interview, and I was soon remembering enough for a third draft to be written, then this, final, account. A lot of my army mates and POW colleagues saw the *Post* article and contacted me. To a man, each of them said, 'Don, I had no idea this had happened to you. Why didn't you tell someone sooner?' They also said, 'Don, your story is mind-blowing. If anyone else had written it, I wouldn't have believed it. But I know you, Don. You're a good and honest man and I believe you.' I found this tremendously gratifying.

So why did I keep all this to myself for so long? The truth is I just wanted to forget about it. When I returned from the war, I had horrible nightmares and bad stomach pains, but instead of getting it out of my system by seeing the authorities and telling them about it, I consciously blocked out every memory. I've always been a strong-willed person (I'm sure this is what helped me survive in Auschwitz), and it was this same strength of mind that enabled me to put all the memories behind me when I returned to Australia. But it came at a price.

Because of these efforts to keep myself under control, it wasn't until 1957 — 12 years after the war — that I was able to go on an Anzac Day parade. I also made a point of avoiding every single prisoner-of-war movie that came along. The fact that I have referred in this book to scenes in *The Great Escape* is because a few people who read the *I Was There Too* booklet told me that certain things I wrote about, such as tunnelling and making clothes and forged documents in the POW camp, had reminded them of the film. Until then, please believe me, I had no idea about the movie or anything it portrayed.

I've been to a number of POW reunions, especially in recent years. I've enjoyed meeting up with men I hadn't seen since the war and hearing how well they've done in civilian life. Unless you have been a serviceman, you can't understand the strong bond that exists between men who have been through a war together. You feel lucky to have survived, and you know that these men will always be the best mates you will ever have. If you are ill and go to hospital, they always find time to visit you, or at least write a note or send a card. I think it's a crying shame that our boys who served in Korea and Vietnam were not shown more respect and gratitude when they returned. To me we are all equal.

As for our former German enemies, there are good and bad soldiers in all armies. A lot of the POW camp guards in World War II were prisoners of war during World War I and were badly treated by the Allies. They were out for revenge. As for the SS guards at Auschwitz, many of them, I'm sure, had been brainwashed into thinking they were superior people who were doing what was best for their country. I'm just as certain that a great many of them were out-and-out sadists who loved every bit of their duties.

In this regard, I feel particularly sorry for people such as English historian David Irving, who have fostered a culture of denial, using their considerable education, intelligence and intellect to claim that the atrocities of the Holocaust did not happen. David Irving's basis for this claim is that he visited Auschwitz and saw no evidence of the gas that was used, and could find no reference in official Nazi records to the mass killings, the genocide, that took place.

Well, of course he couldn't find anything. The Nazis weren't stupid. When they knew they were losing the war in a serious way, and that trials for war crimes were inevitable, they destroyed anything they could find that would have been in the least bit incriminating.

I have no wish to debate the issue with David Irving — after all, he is a highly educated man and a skilled communicator, and I am not. All I can say to him is, 'Mr Irving, I am not Jewish and I am not part of the so-called "Jewish conspiracy". But I was in Belsen, and in Auschwitz, and I can tell you that mass extermination of Jewish people did take place. For you to claim otherwise is insulting. I know this because I was there, stoking the fires. And I saw it happen.'

As I write these concluding words, I sincerely hope that all those of you who were born after World War II never lose sight of what can happen to humanity when a group of fanatics decide to use extreme measures for their own ends. The sad thing about democracies is that it's always their elected leaders who start wars and drag their hapless fellow countrymen into fighting them.

I'm not an educated man, and there's a lot about the world and its ways that I don't know. But I have talked to quite a few people about politics, philosophy and the psychology of evil since starting work on this book, and I've been greatly impressed by a lot of what I have heard. I was particularly taken by Edmund Burke, the 18th-century English philosopher and politician, who felt that democracy wasn't such a good thing, because it gave rise to demagogues.

With that in mind, it is my hope that today's generations, those who are young enough to be my grandchildren and great-grandchildren, can spot a demagogue when one comes along. I also hope they realise that there is no need for wars if commonsense and a concern for fellow human beings are allowed to prevail. Above all, I hope they can hold on to this belief when they themselves become leaders, although recent events in Bosnia, Somalia and Rwanda don't give me much cause of optimism.

As for the atrocities of the Holocaust — if good and

decent people had acted promptly in accordance with their conscience instead of burying their heads in the sand, one of the worst episodes in the history of the world would never have happened. Whenever we see any form of injustice happening to another human being, it is our duty, as fellow human beings, to speak out against it and try to stop it.

I'm not trying to be moralistic or pretend that I'm better than anyone else, but the simple fact is that if we don't speak out against evil and injustice whenever we see it, we really can't complain or call on anyone else for assistance when we ourselves are on the receiving end of injustice and evil.

As Edmund Burke said in one of his most famous quotations: 'The only thing necessary for the triumph of evil is for good men to do nothing.'

I think Edmund Burke got it right.

Don Watt
Tweed Heads
January 1995

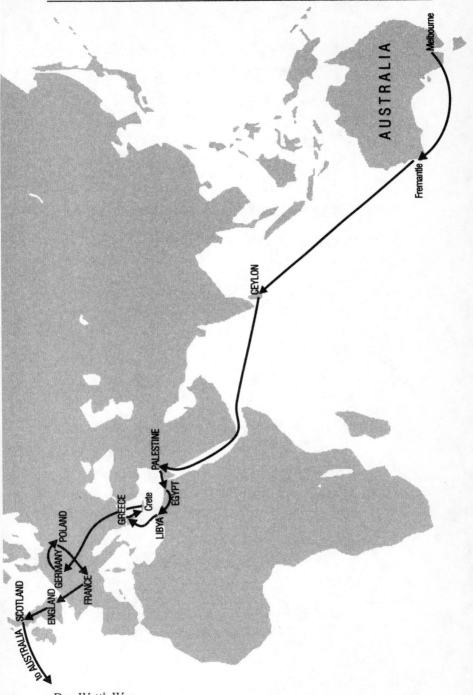

Don Watt's War